P9-BJJ-440

CHINESE COOKING

CHARTWELL
BOOKS INC.

Picture Credits:
Dr Hugh Baker 5.
Camera Press 10.
Douglas Dickens 2/3.
Alan Duns 7, 48, 49, 57, 61.
Melvin Grey 45.
Paul Kemp 21, 36/7.
Marc Riboud/Magnum 1, 4.
David Meldrum 57.
Roger Phillips 8, 13, 15, 16, 22, 27-35, 38. 40, 43,
46/7 52/3, 56/7, 62.
Iain Reid 50, 55, 63.
David Smith 19.
Zefa 24.

Cover: Roger Phillips.

Written and edited by Isabel Moore

Published by Chartwell Books Inc.,
a Division of Book Sales, Inc.,
110 Enterprise Avenue,
Secaucus, New Jersey 07094

© Marshall Cavendish Limited 1973, 1974, 1975, 1977

Parts of this material first published by Marshall
Cavendish Limited in the part work *Supercook*

This volume first published 1977

This edition is not to be sold outside the United
States of America, Canada and the Philippine Republic

Printed in Great Britain

ISBN 0 89009 100 5

Contents

Introduction

The delights of Chinese cooking have only recently become available to the west, but nearly everyone now knows just how good, and how economical, a Chinese meal can be. What is just beginning to be appreciated by the public at large is just how very easy it is to create these same meals, or even better ones, in your own kitchen, so that the joys of eating Chinese-style can be experienced regularly rather than as an occasional treat.

About one-third of the world's population eat Chinese food every day of their lives, yet it is much, much more than the daily sustenance of a great many people. Even if it were only eaten regularly by a handful of obscure gourmets, Chinese cooking would still be important for it is one of the truly great and original cuisines of the world.

The Chinese were a civilized nation long before the ancestors of the western world had advanced to the condition of warring tribes, whose lives consisted mainly of robbery and rape, of killing and hunting. And as the Chinese civilization developed and reached new heights of achievement, so the cuisine became more sophisticated and refined. Since it has always been a large, and rather poor country from an agricultural point of view (only about 12 per cent of it is arable), and since it has always had a very large population to support, there have been many periods of shortage, even starvation. Chinese cooking therefore concentrates on the practical art of making a very little go a very long way, and of making acceptable anything that is edible. And as the cuisine flourished, it became inextricably linked with the philosophy, the religion and the very social fabric of society. Confucius, the man who shaped Chinese life 25 centuries ago, regarded food as a most serious art form. The practice of the art of cooking and of eating was encouraged, and even urged, to round-out the human experience.

China is a vast country, almost equatorial in the south, almost arctic in the north. And in such diverse conditions many different schools of cooking have evolved, although these are usually broken down into five 'classical' regional varieties: Peking and the north, the Yangtze river and the east, Szechuan in the west, Fukien and the southern

coast, and Canton and the south.

Peking has been the capital of China throughout most of its history and it remains one of its great cultural and gastronomic centres. The food of Peking is rich to taste, flavoured with dark, strong soy sauce or paste, and the taste known to the west as sweet and sour is very popular. Garlic is often added to food, and although rice is served, wheat-based dishes such as noodles and dumplings are more common. The area to the north of Peking is the only part of China where lamb or mutton is eaten with any enthusiasm, and the border area with Mongolia is the home of the 'firepot', now an accepted part of the Chinese cooking ritual. The fire pot somewhat resembles the western fondue, and is one of only a few Chinese dishes which are considered to be a meal in themselves.

The eastern part of the Yangtze river includes the cities of Ningpo and Shanghai, the latter being traditionally considered as the most cosmopolitan of Chinese cities. The food tends to saltiness, and is often, in fact, preserved in salt. A lot of fish is eaten since much of the region lies on or near the coast, and rice is the staple accompaniment rather than noodles. The food, even the quickly made stir-fry dishes, is cooked for slightly longer than is usual in other parts of the country since the people prefer their meat and vegetables well done.

Szechuan cooking, from the province of the same name in western China, was virtually unknown in the West until ten or fifteen years ago. Since then, there has been an upsurge

cooked in lavish quantities of soy sauce and called 'red-cooked'—pork and cabbage are two foods considered to be particularly suitable for this treatment.

Cantonese and southern cooking is what most people in the west think of as Chinese cooking, for most of the restaurants and Chinese take-away shops outside China are owned by Cantonese. Many stir-fry dishes originate in Canton for the Cantonese do not like their food to be over-cooked, and light soy sauce predominates rather than the heavier, darker type preferred in the north. Dim sum originated here too, especially the steamed varieties, as did the delicate omelets known as foo yungs. And of course glorious Cantonese Lobster—you will find a slightly simplified version of this magnificent feast dish on page 49.

In China food is expected not just to taste delicious and be sustaining, but also to look attractive, so the preparation and combination of ingredients is important not just from the point of view of taste but also from an aesthetic one. Menus which start with soups and work their way through to desserts are unknown. Instead, depending on the grandness of the occasion, a selection of four, six, eight or up to almost any number of dishes is placed on the table and the diners are expected to help themselves, and in any order they wish. The only 'rule' is that different dishes are not piled on the plate at the same time or otherwise sampled together as is the practice in the west. Each dish is expected to be savoured separately in order to extract the full goodness. Soups are usually eaten as refreshers during the meal, as are sweetmeats.

There are no laws governing what is served with what, but there are philosophical and practical requirements which are taken into account. At a formal feast, for instance, the menu would probably contain an offering from the air (steamed wood pigeons or a birds' nest soup, perhaps), an offering from the sea (some carp, perhaps, or shrimps, a favourite Chinese seafood), and an offering from the land (meat or vegetables). In addition, or as part of the above, there would be an example of sweet and sour, perhaps something cooked in oyster sauce or black bean sauce, an example of stir-fry, one of steaming and one of long, slow cooking, such as a casserole or a roast. The final choice depends, as it has always done, on the capacities of the cook, both in cooking terms and in terms of the availability of money and ingredients.

of interest in it and although there are as yet few restaurants which specialize in the cooking of this region, many predominantly Cantonese or Pekingese restaurants offer one or two specialities from Szechuan—especially the cousin to Peking Duck, Szechuan Duck, or Szechuan Shrimps. It produces by far the hottest, spiciest food in China, almost as hot sometimes as a curry although the taste is very different, and one of the essential ingredients in many of the traditional dishes is chillis. Garlic and ginger are also used to help sharpen the food.

Fukien and the southern coastal lands are also noted for their fish dishes, and Fukien is famous throughout China as producer of the finest soy sauce in the land. As a result of this, many of the most famous local dishes are

Right: *Sowing rice by the traditional methods in Kwangsi Province. Old ways are changing now, however; much of the land is now operated by communes and modern methods are being introduced.*

Far right: *A traditional ceremony of ancestor worship—in this particular feast incense is burnt and a roast pig offered.*

Rice and noodles, the staple foods of China, are not usually served at banquets or formal feasts, simply because they are considered to belong to the everyday, to the necessary, and are not therefore deemed worthy of a 'special' occasion.

Chinese food can be eaten perfectly adequately with western cutlery such as forks and spoons, but it achieves a greater delicacy when eaten with chopsticks, partly because the diner is then forced to eat smaller portions at a time and also more slowly, therefore savouring the food more completely. The legends which surround the origin and the use of chopsticks vary but there is one which suggests that they are wholly practical implements: by eating small morsels at a time you can make a very little go a very long way— often a necessity in China throughout its long history.

Table-setting is simpler than in the west and consists of chopsticks, a selection of bowls of different sizes (for rice, soup, meat dishes, etc), plus a soup spoon, if soup is to be served. If wine or tea is to accompany the meal, an appropriate small cup is added to the table. Napkins, as they are used in the west, are unknown, but, as in Japan, a hot, damp hand towel is handed to guests both before and during the meal. Since the centre of the table is needed for the selection of dishes being presented, there are no floral or other decorations on the Chinese table.

Etiquette, especially for more formal occasions, used to be quite rigid. In contrast to western custom, the pride of place traditionally reserved for the guest of honour was often as far away from the host as it was possible to be, but always directly across from the doorway or opening through which the food would come. Shao Hsing or rice wine is the drink traditionally served at formal feasts, although tea could be served instead.

Tea, in fact, has almost as long and honoured a history in China as it has in Japan and it is surrounded by almost as much ritual. There is even a 'patron saint' of tea! The types most usually served are a version of oolong, or a 'green' (unfermented) tea. Many flowers and leaves, such as jasmine, are also added to give it a special taste. Chinese tea should be served in small handleless cups, without the addition of milk, lemon or sugar.

Preparation of food

In order to produce the beautiful banquets described above, a good deal of preparation is necessary, but basically Chinese cooking is quite simple. The only prerequisite is to be as orderly as possible and to prepare everything you can before the actual cooking process begins. So before you start experimenting with any of the recipes which follow, prepare all of the ingredients, measure them, slice them, chop them, then line them up beside the stove in the order in which they are to be added to the cooking pot. Many dishes, especially the stir-fry ones, just do not allow time to turn around and scramble amid a chaos of half-prepared ingredients.

The secret of Chinese cooking lies, in fact, in the preparation. Food is sliced, shredded or cut according to certain predetermined rules. For really successful short-cooking dishes, all of the ingredients should be cut or chopped to as near the same size as possible to ensure that they are all cooked to the same degree. For very tender, almost velvety meat, the meat should be sliced along the grain; for a slightly crunchier texture it should be sliced against. (Slightly frozen meat is often easier to slice into very thin strips in this way than meat at room temperature.) Vegetables,

4

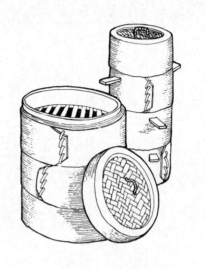

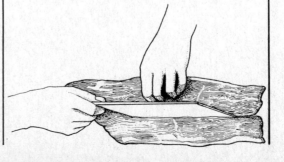

particularly, are often sliced on the diagonal both for aesthetic appeal and for regularity of cooking. The cleaver, an implement indispensable in the Chinese kitchen, is the basic instrument used both to slice and shred food, but you do not have to have one in order to create an authentic Chinese touch—a really sharp knife will do just as well.

The basic traditional Chinese cooking vessel is called a wok, and is a cross between a rather deep frying-pan and a rather shallow saucepan, except that it has sloping sides and a somewhat rounded base. It is available in the west, from larger department stores as well as fancy kitchen shops, and of course can be bought quite cheaply from Chinese provision stores. It is an extremely versatile cooking implement and can be converted very successfully to cooking western food as well as Chinese. The wok is particularly suitable for stir-fry dishes, since its rounded base and sloping sides help to keep the food in motion during the stirring and turning process which is intrinsic to the technique.

The wok is also used as the base for steamed dishes. Traditional flat, round bamboo steamers are fitted over a wok filled with water (they can be stacked on top of each other, up to four or five at a time). However, an ordinary steamer or even a *couscoussier* is equally effective. Food steamed in the bamboo steamers can be served still in the steamers. Shallow perforated spoons, somewhat similar in appearance to bulb basters, are widely used in deep-frying, another popular method of cooking in China; slotted spoons make an acceptable substitute for the western kitchen.

The rewards of cooking Chinese are obvious to anyone who has ever eaten a well-cooked Sweet and Sour Pork, or been sustained by a succulent Chow Mein. Now that you know how easy and economical it can be, Chinese food need never be a once-a-week restaurant treat again!

Some popular cooking aids and techniques from the Chinese kitchen : Top: *The most versatile cooking pot in China, the wok ;* Second from top: *A typical bamboo steamer—food is often served in it as well as cooked ;* Third from top: *A baster, particularly useful for deep-frying ;* Second from bottom: *Cutting vegetables diagonally with a traditional cleaver—it has aesthetic appeal and the even cutting ensures even cooking ;* Bottom: *Cutting meat with the grain, to ensure velvety softness when cooked.*

5

Soups

FOONG YIN MUN SUNG
(Birds' Nest Soup with Chicken Cubes and Mushrooms)

This is one of the classics of Cantonese cuisine and is very filling indeed. Birds' nests and quail eggs can be obtained from oriental or Chinese delicatessens.

	Metric/U.K.	U.S.
Birds' nests	225g/8oz	8oz
Vegetable oil	1 Tbs	1 Tbs
Chopped fresh root ginger	1 Tbs	1 Tbs
Cooked chicken, cubed	125g/4oz	4oz
Button mushrooms, quartered	125g/4oz	4oz
Canned quail eggs, drained	225g/8oz	8oz
Chicken stock	1¾l/3 pints	7½ cups

Soak the birds' nests in water for 5 minutes, then drain.

Heat the oil in a saucepan. Add the ginger and fry for 1 minute, stirring constantly. Stir in the chicken, mushrooms, eggs and stock and bring to the boil. Reduce the heat to low and add the birds' nests. Simmer for 5 minutes, stirring occasionally.

Transfer the soup to a warmed tureen or large bowl and serve at once.

6-8 Servings

EGG-DROP SOUP

	Metric/U.K.	U.S.
Vegetable oil	1 Tbs	1 Tbs
Medium onion, thinly sliced	1	1
Small cucumber, finely diced	1	1
Chicken stock	1¾l/3 pints	7½ cups
Tomatoes, blanched, peeled and quartered	4	4
Egg, lightly beaten	1	1

Heat the oil in a large saucepan. Add the onion and fry for 1 minute, stirring constantly. Add the cucumber to the pan and fry for 1 minute, stirring constantly. Pour over the stock and bring to the boil. Reduce the heat to low and simmer for 10 minutes, stirring occasionally. Stir in the tomatoes and simmer for a further 5 minutes.

Remove from the heat and beat in the egg. Serve at once.

6 Servings

CUCUMBER AND PORK SOUP

	Metric/U.K.	U.S.
Chicken stock	1⅓l/2¼ pints	5¾ cups
Salt	1 tsp	1 tsp
Soy sauce	1 Tbs	1 Tbs
Pork fillet (tenderloin), cut into very thin strips	225g/8oz	8oz
Medium cucumbers, peeled, halved lengthways, seeded and cut into ½cm/¼in slices	2	2

Pour the stock, salt and soy sauce into a large saucepan and stir in the pork strips. Bring to the boil over moderate heat and cook for 10 minutes. Add the cucumbers to the pan and return to the boil. Cook for 3 minutes, or until the cucumbers are translucent.

Transfer the soup to a warmed tureen and serve at once.

4 Servings

CRABMEAT SOUP

	Metric/U.K.	U.S.
Water	250ml/8floz	1 cup
Medium onion, chopped	1	1
Fresh root ginger, peeled and halved lengthways	2½cm/1in piece	1in piece
Chicken stock	300ml/10floz	1¼ cups
Crabmeat with the shell and cartilage removed	½kg/1lb	1lb

Salt	1 tsp	1 tsp
Rice wine or dry sherry	3 Tbs	3 Tbs
Chicken stock cube, crumbled	$\frac{1}{2}$	$\frac{1}{2}$
Cornflour (cornstarch)	$1\frac{1}{2}$ Tbs	$1\frac{1}{2}$ Tbs
Milk	300ml/10floz	$1\frac{1}{4}$ cups
Vegetable fat, cut into small cubes	2 tsp	2 tsp

Pour the water into a saucepan and set over moderate heat. Add the onion and ginger and boil until the liquid has been reduced by half. Add the stock, crabmeat, salt and wine or sherry. Reduce the heat to moderately low and slowly bring to the boil, skimming off any scum which rises to the surface.

Blend the stock cube and cornflour (cornstarch) with the milk until smooth and pour into the soup, stirring constantly until the soup has thickened and is smooth. Cook for 2 minutes, stirring constantly, or until the soup is hot but not boiling. Sprinkle over the vegetable fat.

Transfer the soup to a warmed tureen and serve at once.

6 Servings

HOT AND SOUR SOUP

This soup is a speciality of the province of Szechuan in western China and has a most unusual but very attractive taste. Sesame oil can be obtained from health food or Chinese provision stores.

Cucumber and Pork Soup —light, delicious and so easy and quick to make.

	Metric/U.K.	U.S.
Sesame oil	2 Tbs	2 Tbs
Medium onions, finely chopped	2	2
Flour	2 Tbs	2 Tbs
Chicken stock	$1\frac{1}{4}$l/2 pints	5 cups
Juice of 1 lemon		
Soy sauce	2 Tbs	2 Tbs
Monosodium glutamate (MSG), (optional)	$\frac{1}{4}$ tsp	$\frac{1}{4}$ tsp
Salt and pepper to taste		
Bean sprouts	275g/10oz	10oz
Chinese dried mushrooms, soaked in cold water for 20 minutes, drained and chopped	2	2
Canned bamboo shoot, drained and finely chopped	125g/4oz	4oz
Cooked chicken, finely diced	125g/4oz	4oz

Heat the oil in a large saucepan. Add the onions and fry until they are soft. Remove from the heat and stir in the flour to form a smooth paste. Gradually stir in the remaining ingredients until they are well blended and the mixture is smooth. Return the pan to moderate heat and bring to the boil, stirring constantly. Cover the pan, reduce the heat to low and simmer for 1 hour.

Transfer the soup to a warmed tureen and serve at once.

6 Servings

Huang Yu Tang is a traditional and unusual soup in which the fish is first deep-fried then served with a delicious broth.

HUANG YU TANG (Fish Soup)

	Metric/U.K.	U.S.
Herrings or trout, cleaned and boned	½kg/1lb	1lb
Salt	1½ tsp	1½ tsp
Ground ginger	1½ tsp	1½ tsp
Vinegar	2 Tbs	2 Tbs
Sufficient vegetable oil for deep-frying		
Boiling water	900ml/ 1½ pints	3¾ cups
Chicken stock cube	1	1
Soy sauce	1½ Tbs	1½ Tbs
Watercress, stalks removed	1 bunch	1 bunch
Rice wine or dry sherry	2 Tbs	2 Tbs
Black pepper	½ tsp	½ tsp

Rub the insides and outsides of the fish with salt, ginger and half the vinegar. Set aside to marinate for 1 hour. Drain the fish and pat dry with kitchen towels.

Fill a large saucepan one-third full with vegetable oil and heat until it reaches 185°C (360°F) on a deep-fat thermometer, or until a small cube of stale bread dropped into the oil turns golden in 50 seconds. Arrange the fish in a deep-frying basket and carefully lower them into the oil. Fry for 5 to 6 minutes, or until they are crisp. Remove from the oil and drain on kitchen towels.

Put the fish in a large saucepan and pour over the boiling water. Crumble in the stock cube and add the remaining vinegar and the soy sauce. Bring to the boil, reduce the heat to moderately low and simmer for 5 minutes. Carefully stir in the remaining ingredients.

Transfer the soup to a warmed tureen and serve at once.

4 Servings

WONTON DOUGH

Roll out the dough very thinly, to not more than about ⅛cm/ 1/16 in thick, then cut into shapes as you require (the most usual ones are rectangles or squares).

	Metric/U.K.	U.S.
Flour	450g/1lb	4 cups
Salt	2 tsp	2 tsp

	Metric/U.K.	U.S.
Eggs, lightly beaten	2	2
Water	75ml/3floz	$\frac{3}{8}$ cup

Sift the flour and salt into a bowl. Make a well in the centre and pour in the eggs and water. Using your fingers or a spatula, draw the flour into the liquid until it has been incorporated and the dough comes away from the sides of the bowl.

Turn the dough out on to a lightly floured surface and knead for 10 minutes, or until it is smooth and elastic.

The dough is now ready to use.

Enough dough for 72 wrappers

WONTON SOUP

Wonton wrappers can be bought at most Chinese delicatessens, or they can be made according to the recipe for Wonton dough above.

	Metric/U.K.	U.S.
Lean beef, minced (ground)	$\frac{1}{2}$kg/1lb	1lb
Soy sauce	2 Tbs	2 Tbs
Fresh root ginger, peeled and finely chopped	2$\frac{1}{2}$cm/1in piece	1in piece
Salt	1 tsp	1 tsp
Grated nutmeg	1 tsp	1 tsp
Chopped spinach	275g/10oz	1$\frac{2}{3}$ cups
Wonton dough, thinly rolled and cut into 36 squares, or 36 bought wonton wrappers	225g/8oz	8oz
Chicken stock	1$\frac{3}{4}$l/3 pints	7$\frac{1}{2}$ cups
Watercress, chopped	1 bunch	1 bunch

Put the beef, soy sauce, ginger, salt, nutmeg and spinach in a bowl and mix thoroughly until they are well blended.

Lay the wrappers on a flat surface and put a little filling just below the centre. Wet the edges of the dough, then fold over one corner to make a triangle, pinching the edges together to seal. Pull the corners at the base of the triangle together and pinch to seal.

Half-fill a large saucepan with water and bring to the boil. Drop in the wontons and return to the boil. Cook for 5 minutes, or until the wontons are tender but still firm. Remove from the heat and pour off the water. Return the wontons to the pan and pour in the stock.

Bring to the boil, then stir in the watercress. Return to the boil.

Transfer the soup to a warmed tureen and serve at once.

6 Servings

YU-CHI-TANG (Shark's Fin Soup)

This is one of the great festive dishes of China and is served on special occasions.

	Metric/U.K.	U.S.
Sesame oil	2 Tbs	2 Tbs
Spring onion (scallion), finely chopped	1	1
Fresh root ginger, peeled and finely chopped	2$\frac{1}{2}$cm/1in piece	1in piece
Chinese dried mushrooms, soaked in cold water for 20 minutes, drained and sliced	4	4
Rice wine or dry sherry	2 Tbs	2 Tbs
Chicken stock	2l/3$\frac{1}{2}$ pints	2$\frac{1}{4}$ quarts
Ready-prepared shark's fin, soaked for 1 hour in cold water and drained	125g/4oz	4oz
Boned chicken breast, shredded	225g/8oz	8oz
Peeled small prawns or shrimps	225g/8oz	8oz
Soy sauce	1$\frac{1}{2}$ Tbs	1$\frac{1}{2}$ Tbs
Cornflour (cornstarch), blended with 1 Tbs chicken stock	1$\frac{1}{2}$ Tbs	1$\frac{1}{2}$ Tbs

Heat the oil in a large saucepan. Add the spring onion (scallion), ginger, mushrooms and wine or sherry and fry for 5 minutes, stirring occasionally. Pour over half the chicken stock, add the shark's fin and bring to the boil. Reduce the heat to low and simmer for 10 minutes. Add the chicken, prawns or shrimps and soy sauce. Pour in the remaining chicken stock and the cornflour (cornstarch) mixture, and bring to the boil, stirring constantly. Reduce the heat to low and simmer for a further 10 minutes, stirring occasionally. Serve at once.

8-10 Servings

Firepots are Mongolian in origin but they have been adopted (and improved) by the Chinese and are now a great favourite. This particular version is a rich meal in itself, but you can if you wish make a more modest version by omitting some of the garnishes and serving less expensive fish.

CHICKEN VEGETABLE FIREPOT

'Firepots' are the Chinese equivalent of fondues— the main offering is cooked in a central 'pot' at the table and eaten with garnishes and side dishes grouped around the central dish. This is a simplified version of a Mongolian dish.

	Metric/U.K.	U.S.
Roasting chicken	1x2kg/4lb	1x4lb
Onion, chopped	1	1
Bouquet garni	1	1
Peppercorns	10	10
Bay leaves	2	2
Salt	1 tsp	1 tsp
Water	1¼l/2 pints	5 cups
Lobster meat	175g/6oz	6oz
Large prawns (shrimps), shelled	175g/6oz	6oz
VEGETABLES		
Mushrooms, sliced or whole if small	125g/4oz	4oz
Red pepper, pith and seeds removed and sliced	1	1
Green pepper, pith and seeds removed and sliced	1	1
Celery or Chinese		

	Metric/U.K.	U.S.
cabbage, thinly sliced or shredded	125g/4oz	4oz
Canned water chestnuts, drained and sliced or lotus root, sliced	125g/4oz	4oz
GARNISHES Cooked rice	275g/10oz	4 cups
Chopped spring onions (scallions)	4 Tbs	4 Tbs
Fresh root ginger, peeled and finely chopped	10cm/4in piece	4in piece
Chopped parsley or coriander	4 Tbs	4 Tbs

Remove the skin, bones and flesh from the chicken. Set the flesh aside and put the skin, bones and any giblets into a saucepan with the onion, bouquet garni, peppercorns, bay leaves, salt and water. Bring to the boil, skimming off any scum that rises to the surface. Cover the pan, reduce the heat to low and simmer the stock for 1 to 1½ hours. Remove from the heat and strain. Set the stock aside.

Meanwhile, prepare the meat and fish. Cut the chicken flesh into small bite-sized pieces and arrange decoratively on a large serving dish. Cut the lobster meat and prawns (shrimps) into bite-sized pieces and arrange decoratively with the chicken. Set aside.

To prepare the vegetables, arrange them attractively on a large serving platter and set them aside with the meat and fish.

Put all the garnishes in separate bowls (dividing the rice into individual-bowl servings) and arrange with the other dishes.

Put the fondue or firepot in the centre of the table and arrange the platters around it. Light the spirit burner and pour the boiling stock into the pot. The food is now ready to be cooked, in the same way as fondue.

6 Servings

WONTONS WITH PORK AND SHRIMPS

	Metric/U.K.	U.S.
Vegetable oil	2 Tbs	2 Tbs
Lean pork, minced (ground)	225g/8oz	8oz
Peeled shrimps, finely chopped	225g/8oz	8oz
Soy sauce	2 Tbs	2 Tbs
Rice wine or dry sherry	1 Tbs	1 Tbs
Salt	½ tsp	½ tsp
Bamboo shoots, finely chopped	2 Tbs	2 Tbs
Chinese dried mushrooms, soaked in cold water for 20 minutes, drained and chopped	2	2
Spring onions (scallions), finely chopped	2	2
Cornflour (cornstarch), blended with 1 Tbs water	1 tsp	1 tsp
Wonton dough, thinly rolled and cut into 36 squares, or 36 bought wonton wrappers	225g/8oz	8oz
Sufficient vegetable oil for deep-frying		

Heat the oil in a frying-pan. Add the pork and fry until it loses its pinkness. Stir in the shrimps, soy sauce, wine or sherry, salt, bamboo shoots and vegetables and fry for 1 minute, stirring constantly. Stir in the cornflour (cornstarch) mixture until the pan mixture thickens. Remove from the heat, transfer to a bowl and set aside to cool.

Lay the wrappers on a flat surface and put a little filling just below the centre. Wet the edges of the dough, then fold over one corner to make a triangle, pinching the edges together to seal. Pull the corners at the base of the triangle together and pinch to seal.

Fill a large saucepan one-third full with oil and heat until it reaches 190°C (375°F) on a deep-fat thermometer, or until a small cube of stale bread dropped into the oil turns golden in 40 seconds. Carefully lower the wontons into the oil, a few at a time, and fry for 2 to 3 minutes, or until they are golden brown. Remove from the oil and drain on kitchen towels.

Transfer the wontons to a warmed serving dish and serve piping hot.

8 Servings

SHRIMP DUMPLNGS

	Metric/U.K.	U.S.
Shelled shrimps	225g/8oz	8oz

Dim Sum are Cantonese in origin and in and around Canton, a selection of them are often eaten as a whole meal. The two dim sums pictured here are both steamed dim sums—Shrimp Dumplings on the left and Feng Kuo (crabmeat dumplings) on the right.

Spring onions (scallions), finely chopped	2	2
Chopped bean sprouts	2 Tbs	2 Tbs
Soy sauce	2 tsp	2 tsp
Rice wine or dry sherry	1 tsp	1 tsp
Sugar	¼ tsp	¼ tsp
DUMPLINGS		
Flour	225g/8oz	2 cups
Hot water	125ml/4floz	½ cup

To make the dumplings, sift the flour into a large bowl. Make a well in the centre and pour in the water. Using your fingers or a spatula, draw the flour into the liquid until it has been incorporated and the dough comes away from the sides of the bowl. Turn the dough out on to a lightly floured surface and knead for 5 minutes, or until it is smooth and elastic. Return to the bowl, cover and set aside for 30 minutes.

Chop the shrimps finely and transfer them to a bowl. Stir in the spring onions (scallions), bean sprouts, soy sauce, wine or dry sherry and sugar until the mixture is thoroughly blended.

Turn the dough out on to the floured surface and roll out into a sausage about 2½cm/1in in diameter. Cut the dough into slices about 2½cm/1in wide. Flatten the slices evenly with your fingers until they measure about 7½cm/3in in diameter.

Place a teaspoon of filling in the centre of each dough circle. Gather up the dough around the filling and bring it up and over, pleating it slightly as you bring it towards the centre. Turn the ends clockwise slightly to seal the filling in completely.

Half-fill a large saucepan or the bottom half of a steamer with water. Bring to the boil over high heat. Arrange the dumplings in a colander or the top half of the steamer, sealed side up, and place over the boiling water. Reduce the heat to moderate and steam the dumplings for about 10 minutes.

Transfer to a warmed serving dish and serve at once.

4-6 Servings

FENG KUO (Crabmeat Dumplings)

	Metric/U.K.	U.S.
Vegetable oil	2 Tbs	2 Tbs
Chopped spring onions (scallions)	1 Tbs	1 Tbs
Finely chopped fresh root ginger	1 Tbs	1 Tbs
Chinese dried mushrooms, soaked in cold water for 20 minutes, drained and chopped	6	6
Crabmeat, shell and cartilage removed and flaked	225g/8oz	8oz
Salt and pepper to taste		
Sugar	¼ tsp	¼ tsp
Soy sauce	1 tsp	1 tsp
Rice wine or dry sherry	1 Tbs	1 Tbs
DUMPLINGS		
Flour	225g/8oz	2 cups
Hot water	125ml/4floz	½ cup

To make the dumplings, sift the flour into a large bowl. Make a well in the centre and pour in the water. Using your fingers or a spatula, draw the flour into the liquid until it has been incorporated and the dough comes away from the sides of the bowl. Turn the dough out on to a lightly floured surface and knead for 5 minutes, or until it is smooth and elastic. Return to the bowl, cover and set aside for 30 minutes.

Heat the oil in a large frying-pan. Add the spring onions (scallions), ginger, mushrooms and crabmeat and stir-fry for 3 minutes. Stir in the remaining ingredients and fry for a further 1 minute, stirring constantly. Remove from the heat and set aside.

Turn the dough out on to the floured surface and roll out into a sausage about 2½cm/1in in diameter. Cut the dough into slices about 2½cm/1in wide. Flatten the slices evenly with your fingers until they measure about 7½cm/3in in diameter.

Place a teaspoon of filling on one side of each dough circle. Fold over the circles to make a semi-circle and pinch to seal.

Half-fill a large saucepan or the bottom half of a steamer with water. Bring to the boil over high heat. Arrange the dumplings in a colander or the top half of the steamer and place over the boiling water. Reduce the heat to moderate and steam the dumplings for about 10 minutes.

Transfer to a warmed serving dish and serve at once.

4-6 Servings

Meins and Foo Yungs

heat to high. Fry for 1 minute, stirring constantly, adding more oil or soy sauce to the pan if necessary. Spoon the bean and chicken mixture over the pasta and serve at once.

4-6 Servings

CHOW MEIN (Fried Noodles)

This is the basic and probably one of the most popular of the Chinese noodle dishes.

	Metric/U.K.	U.S.
Egg noodles or spaghetti	½kg/1lb	1lb
French (green) beans	225g/8oz	8oz
Vegetable oil	50ml/2floz	¼ cup
Medium onion, thinly sliced	1	1
Garlic clove, crushed	1	1
Chicken meat, finely shredded	125g/4oz	4oz
Soy sauce	2 Tbs	2 Tbs
Sugar	1 tsp	1 tsp
Rice wine or dry sherry	1 Tbs	1 Tbs
Butter	1½ Tbs	1½ Tbs
Chicken stock	3 Tbs	3 Tbs
Chicken stock cube, crumbled	½	½

Cook the noodles or spaghetti in boiling, salted water until they are just tender. Drain, set aside and keep hot. Cook the beans in boiling, salted water for 5 minutes. Drain, set aside and keep hot.

Heat the oil in a large frying-pan. Add the onion and garlic and fry for 2 minutes, stirring constantly. Add the chicken and stir-fry for 1 minute. Add the beans, soy sauce, sugar and wine or sherry and stir-fry for a further 1 minute. Using a slotted spoon, transfer the bean and chicken mixture to a bowl. Keep hot.

Add the butter, stock and stock cube to the oil in the pan. Add the noodles or pasta and fry for 2 minutes, stirring and turning constantly. Add half the bean and chicken mixture. Transfer the mixture to a warmed serving dish, set aside and keep hot.

Return the remaining bean and chicken mixture to the frying-pan and increase the

PRAWN OR SHRIMP CHOW MEIN

	Metric/U.K.	U.S.
Peanut oil for deep-frying		
Thin egg noodles, cooked and drained	225g/8oz	8oz
Vegetable oil	2 Tbs	2 Tbs
Chinese dried mushrooms, soaked in cold water for 20 minutes, drained and sliced	10	10
Carrots, thinly sliced on the diagonal	2	2
Bean sprouts	225g/8oz	8oz
Canned water chestnuts, drained and sliced	225g/8oz	8oz
Chicken stock	125ml/4floz	½ cup
Rice wine or dry sherry	1 Tbs	1 Tbs
Soy sauce	1 Tbs	1 Tbs
Prawns or shrimps, shelled	350g/12oz	12oz

Fill a large saucepan one-third full with oil and heat until it reaches 185°C (360°F) on a deep-fat thermometer, or until a small cube of stale bread dropped into the oil turns golden in 50 seconds. Drop the noodles into the oil and fry for 3 to 4 minutes or until they are golden brown. Remove from the oil and drain on kitchen towels. Arrange the noodles on a serving dish and keep hot while you make the sauce.

Heat the oil in a large frying-pan. Add the vegetables and fry until they are tender but crisp. Stir in the stock and wine or sherry and bring to the boil. Reduce the heat to low and stir in the remaining ingredients. Cover and cook for 3 to 5 minutes, or until the prawns or shrimps are heated through.

Remove from the heat. Pour the sauce over the noodles and serve at once.

3-4 Servings

Noodles are one of the staples of northern China and there are endless delicious recipes based on them. Prawn or Shrimp Chow Mein is one particularly tasty variation.

TAN MEIN (Soup Noodles)

Tan mein is eaten all over China, and primarily as a main or noodle course rather than as a soup course, despite the name.

	Metric/U.K.	U.S.
Egg noodles or spaghetti	350g/12oz	12oz
Vegetable oil	1½ Tbs	1½ Tbs
Small onion, thinly sliced	1	1
Fresh root ginger, peeled and finely chopped	4cm/1½in piece	1½in piece
Lean pork, finely shredded	225g/8oz	8oz
Butter	1 Tbs	1 Tbs
Mushrooms	125g/4oz	4oz
Chinese or white cabbage, blanched for 4 minutes and shredded	125g/4oz	4oz
Bean sprouts, blanched for 1 minute and drained	125g/4oz	4oz
Shrimps or prawns, shelled	125g/4oz	4oz
Soy sauce	1½ Tbs	1½ Tbs
Sugar	1 tsp	1 tsp
Water	300ml/10floz	1¼ cups
Chicken stock cube, crumbled	1	1
Chicken stock	600ml/1 pint	2½ cups

Cook the noodles or spaghetti in boiling, salted water until they are just tender. Drain, set aside and keep hot.

Heat the oil in a large frying-pan. Add the onion, ginger and pork and fry for 2 minutes, stirring constantly. Stir in the butter until it melts. Add the vegetables and shrimps or prawns and fry for 1½ minutes, stirring constantly. Stir in the soy sauce and sugar and stir-fry for a further 1½ minutes. Remove the frying-pan from the heat, set it aside and keep hot.

Pour the water into a saucepan and bring to the boil. Crumble in the stock cube and stir to dissolve it. Add half the pork mixture and the stock and bring the mixture to the boil. Stir in the noodles or spaghetti and simmer for 3 minutes.

Meanwhile, return the frying-pan to high heat and stir-fry the remaining pork mixture for 1 minute to reheat it.

Divide the noodle or spaghetti mixture between four or six individual bowls. Spoon over the remaining pork mixture and serve at once.

4-6 Servings

CHA CHIANG MEIN
(Noodles in Meat Sauce with Shredded Vegetables)

This is one of the classic peasant dishes of Peking and, unlike most Chinese dishes, is a meal in itself. Traditionally, each diner is given a bowl of noodles to which he adds as much meat sauce and shredded vegetables as he likes.

	Metric/U.K.	U.S.
Noodles or spaghetti	½kg/1lb	1lb
Vegetable oil	3 Tbs	3 Tbs
Medium onion, thinly sliced	1	1
Garlic cloves, crushed	2	2
Fresh root ginger, peeled and finely chopped	4cm/1½in piece	1½in piece
Lean pork or beef, minced (ground)	350g/12oz	12oz
Sesame oil	1 Tbs	1 Tbs
Soy sauce	5 Tbs	5 Tbs
Rice wine or dry sherry	2 Tbs	2 Tbs
Sugar	1 Tbs	1 Tbs
Cornflour (cornstarch), blended with 4 Tbs chicken stock	1 Tbs	1 Tbs
SHREDDED VEGETABLES		
Shredded cabbage, blanched for 4 minutes and drained (a heaped side-dishful)	75-125g/3-4oz	3-4oz
Shredded carrots, blanched for 4 minutes and drained (a heaped side-dishful)	75-125g/3-4oz	3-4oz
Bean sprouts, blanched for 1 minute and drained (a heaped side-dishful)	75-125g/3-4oz	3-4oz
Shredded cucumber (a heaped side-dishful)	75-125g/3-4oz	3-4oz
Shredded radishes (a saucerful)	50-75g/2-3oz	4-6 Tbs

Two authentic—and filling—noodle dishes, Tan Mein or soup noodles, and the classic Peking dish Cha Chiang Mein, noodles with meat sauce served with a selection of vegetables and flavourings.

Mixed pickles		
(a saucerful)	25-50g/1-2oz	2-4 Tbs
Chutney (a saucerful)	25-50g/1-2oz	2-4 Tbs

Arrange the shredded vegetables, pickles and chutney on individual serving dishes. Set aside.

Cook the noodles or spaghetti in boiling, salted water until they are just tender. Drain, set aside and keep hot.

Heat the vegetable oil in a large frying-pan. Add the onion, garlic and ginger and fry for 1½ minutes, stirring constantly. Add the pork or beef and stir-fry until it loses its pinkness. Stir in the sesame oil, soy sauce, wine or sherry and sugar, and stir-fry for a further 3 minutes. Stir in the cornflour (cornstarch) mixture and cook, stirring constantly, until the sauce thickens and becomes translucent. Remove from the heat and transfer the sauce to a warmed serving bowl. Keep hot.

Divide the noodles or spaghetti between four individual serving bowls. Serve at once, with the meat sauce and shredded vegetables.

4 Servings

STIR-FRIED BEEF WITH TRANSPARENT NOODLES

	Metric/U.K.	U.S.
Fillet of beef, cut with the grain into thin strips	½kg/1lb	1lb
Soy sauce	3 Tbs	3 Tbs
Rice wine or dry sherry	1 Tbs	1 Tbs
Peanut oil	75ml/3floz	⅜ cup
Cornflour (cornstarch)	2 Tbs	2 Tbs
Transparent noodles	225g/8oz	8oz
Fresh root ginger, peeled and chopped	4cm/1½in piece	1½in piece
Chinese cabbage, shredded	125g/4oz	4oz
Bean sprouts	125g/4oz	4oz
Spring onions (scallions), finely chopped	2	2
Sugar	1½ tsp	1½ tsp
Salt	1 tsp	1 tsp
Beef stock	50ml/2floz	¼ cup

Put the beef strips into a shallow bowl. Combine 2 tablespoons of soy sauce, the wine or sherry, 1 tablespoon of oil and the cornflour (cornstarch) until they are well blended. Pour the mixture over the beef strips and toss gently to coat them. Set aside to marinate at room temperature for 1 hour.

Meanwhile, turn the noodles into a bowl and pour over enough boiling water to cover completely. Set aside to soak for 5 minutes. Drain.

Heat the remaining oil in a very large frying-pan. Add the ginger and beef strips and stir-fry over high heat for 3 minutes. Push the strips to the side of the pan and add the noodles and remaining ingredients. Fry for 2 minutes, then stir the beef strips into the noodles. Add the remaining soy sauce and fry for a further 2 minutes, stirring frequently.

Transfer the mixture to a warmed serving dish and serve at once.

4 Servings

EGG FOO YUNG

This is the Chinese version of the western omelet. It is usually served either on its own (or with a filling, as the following recipe), or it can be cut into strips and stirred into fried rice as a garnish.

	Metric/U.K.	U.S.
Eggs	4	4
Soy sauce	1 Tbs	1 Tbs
Salt and pepper to taste		
Butter	25g/1oz	2 Tbs
Shallot, very finely chopped	1	1
Bean sprouts	125g/4oz	4oz
Cooked ham, cut into thin strips	50g/2oz	2oz

Beat the eggs, soy sauce and seasoning together until the mixture is light and fluffy.

Melt the butter in a frying-pan. Add the shallot, bean sprouts and ham and fry for 4 to 5 minutes, stirring occasionally. Pour in the egg mixture, stir with a fork and leave to set.

Preheat the grill (broiler) to high.

When the bottom of the omelet is set and golden, transfer the pan to the grill (broiler) and grill (broil) until the top is set and lightly browned.

Serve at once, cut into wedges.

2-3 Servings

SHRIMP EGG FOO YUNG

This particular version of foo yung is crisp, filled with succulent chopped shrimps and is served with a delicate sauce.

	Metric/U.K.	U.S.
Vegetable oil	3 Tbs	3 Tbs
Shelled shrimps, chopped	225g/8oz	8oz
Mushrooms, sliced	125g/4oz	4oz
Bean sprouts	125g/4oz	4oz
Eggs, lightly beaten	4	4
SAUCE		
Chicken stock	250ml/8floz	1 cup
Soy sauce	2 tsp	2 tsp
Salt	$\frac{1}{4}$ tsp	$\frac{1}{4}$ tsp
Cornflour (cornstarch), blended with 1 Tbs water	1 Tbs	1 Tbs

Heat 1 tablespoon of oil in a frying-pan. Add the shrimps and stir-fry for 3 minutes, or until they are heated through. Remove from the heat and set aside.

To make the sauce, combine all the ingredients in a small saucepan and bring to the boil, stirring constantly. Cook for 1 minute, stirring constantly, or until the sauce thickens and becomes translucent. Remove the pan from the heat and set aside.

Combine the vegetables, eggs and shrimps in a large bowl and beat until thoroughly blended.

Return the frying-pan to moderate heat and add the remaining oil. When it is hot, add a quarter of the egg mixture and cook for 1 minute or until the bottom is set and golden brown. Turn the omelet over and cook for a further 1 minute, or until it is just set. Transfer to a serving dish and keep hot while you cook the remaining mixture in the same way, to make three more omelets.

Return the pan with the sauce to the heat and bring to the boil, stirring constantly. Pour a little sauce over the omelets and serve at once, with the remaining sauce.

4 Servings

The Chinese version of the western omelet, but much more delicate and crisp. This particular version is Shrimp Egg Foo Yung.

Meat and Poultry

K'OU TSE NGIU LAN
(Leg of Beef in Fruit Sauce)

	Metric/U.K.	U.S.
Vegetable oil	2 Tbs	2 Tbs
Medium onion, thinly sliced	1	1
Garlic cloves, crushed	2	2
Fresh root ginger, peeled and finely chopped	2½cm/1in piece	1in piece
Boned leg (shin) of beef, cubed	1½kg/3lb	3lb
Juice of 1 lemon		
Juice of 2 oranges		
Soy sauce	4 Tbs	4 Tbs
Dry red wine	300ml/10floz	1¼ cups
Water	600ml/1 pint	2½ cups
Salt and pepper to taste		

Preheat the oven to cool 150°C (Gas Mark 2, 300°F).

Heat the oil in a large flameproof casserole. Add the onion, garlic and ginger and stir-fry for 1 minute. Add the beef and fry until it is evenly browned. Stir in all the remaining ingredients and bring to the boil. Transfer the casserole to the oven and bake for 4 hours, stirring three or four times during the cooking period.

Remove from the oven and serve at once.

6-8 Servings

HAO YIU NGIU JOU PIEN
(Quick-Fried Sliced Beef in Oyster Sauce)

	Metric/U.K.	U.S.
Fillet steak, cut into thin strips about 5cm/ 2in x 2½cm/1in	700g/1½lb	1½lb
Salt and white pepper to taste		
Ground ginger	¼ tsp	¼ tsp
Cornflour (cornstarch)	1 Tbs	1 Tbs
Soy sauce	1 Tbs	1 Tbs
Oyster sauce	2½ Tbs	2½ Tbs
Sugar	1 tsp	1 tsp
Rice wine or dry sherry	2 Tbs	2 Tbs
Vegetable oil	75ml/3floz	6 Tbs
Medium onion, thinly sliced	1	1
Garlic clove, crushed	1	1

Rub the beef strips with the salt, pepper, ginger and cornflour (cornstarch).

Combine the soy sauce, oyster sauce, sugar and wine or sherry. Set aside.

Heat the oil in a large frying-pan. Add the onion and garlic and fry for 30 seconds, stirring constantly. Add the beef strips and fry for 2 minutes, stirring constantly. Pour off all but a thin film of oil from the pan. Pour in the reserved sauce and cook for a further 1½ minutes, stirring constantly.

Transfer the mixture to a warmed serving dish and serve at once.

4 Servings

GINGER BEEF

	Metric/U.K.	U.S.
Fillet or rump steak, sliced with the grain into thin strips	½kg/1lb	1lb
Salt and pepper to taste		
Ground ginger	1 tsp	1 tsp
Cornflour (cornstarch)	2 Tbs	2 Tbs
Sesame oil	50ml/2floz	¼ cup
Fresh root ginger, peeled and finely chopped	25g/1oz	3 Tbs
Chopped spring onions (scallions)	2 Tbs	2 Tbs

Put the beef strips in a shallow bowl. Rub them with salt, pepper, ginger and cornflour (cornstarch) and set aside for 10 minutes.

Heat the oil in a frying-pan. Add the root ginger and stir-fry for 2 minutes. Add the beef strips and stir-fry for 3 to 5 minutes, or until they are cooked through.

Unusual but delicious, K'ou Tse Ngiu Lan is leg of beef slowly casseroled in a sauce of fruit and red wine.

Beef with Broccoli takes only a few minutes to cook and the result not only looks fantastic but tastes superb too.

Transfer the strips to a warmed serving dish and sprinkle over the spring onions (scallions). Serve at once.

4 Servings

BEEF WITH BROCCOLI

	Metric/U.K.	U.S.
Fillet of beef, thinly sliced with the grain into 7½cm/3in x 5cm/2in pieces	½kg/1lb	1lb
Soy sauce	3 Tbs	3 Tbs
Rice wine or dry sherry	1 Tbs	1 Tbs
Fresh root ginger, peeled and chopped	2½cm/1in piece	1 in piece
Vegetable oil	50ml/2floz	¼ cup
Broccoli, broken into flowerets	½kg/1lb	1lb

	Metric/U.K.	U.S.
Beef stock	75ml/3floz	$\frac{3}{8}$ cup
Vegetable fat	1 Tbs	1 Tbs
Cornflour (cornstarch), blended with 4 Tbs water	2 tsp	2 tsp

Put the beef strips into a shallow bowl. Combine the soy sauce, wine or sherry, ginger and 1 tablespoon of oil together, then pour over the strips, basting to coat them thoroughly. Set aside to marinate for 15 minutes, stirring and basting occasionally. Meanwhile, cut the broccoli into bite-sized pieces.

Heat the remaining oil in a frying-pan. Add the beef mixture and stir-fry for $1\frac{1}{2}$ minutes. Using a slotted spoon, transfer the beef strips to a plate. Add the stock to the pan and bring to the boil. Add the broccoli and cook for 1 minute, stirring constantly. Reduce the heat to low, cover and simmer the mixture for 4 minutes. Using the slotted spoon, transfer the broccoli to a warmed serving dish. Keep hot.

Add the vegetable fat to the pan and melt it. Return the beef strips to the pan and stir-fry for 30 seconds. Add the cornflour (cornstarch) mixture and stir-fry for 1 minute, or until the sauce becomes translucent. Remove from the heat.

Arrange the beef strips over the broccoli, then pour over the sauce. Serve at once.

4 Servings

CHING-CHIAO-CHAO NIU-JOU
(Steak with Pepper)

	Metric/U.K.	U.S.
Butter	50g/2oz	4 Tbs
Garlic clove, crushed	1	1
Salt and pepper to taste		
Topside (top round) of beef, cut $2\frac{1}{2}$cm/1in thick then into strips●	$\frac{1}{2}$kg/1lb	1lb
Soy sauce	4 Tbs	4 Tbs
Sugar	2 tsp	2 tsp
Bean sprouts	175g/6oz	6oz
Tomatoes, blanched, peeled and quartered	2	2
Green peppers, pith and seeds removed and thinly sliced	2	2
Cornflour (cornstarch), blended with 2 Tbs water	$\frac{1}{2}$ Tbs	$\frac{1}{2}$ Tbs
Spring onions (scallions), sliced	4	4

Melt the butter in a large frying-pan. Add the garlic, salt and pepper and stir-fry for 30 seconds. Add the beef strips and stir-fry for 3 minutes. Increase the heat to high. Stir in the soy sauce and sugar, cover and cook for 5 minutes. Uncover, and stir in the bean sprouts, tomatoes and peppers. Re-cover and simmer for 5 minutes. Stir in the cornflour (cornstarch) mixture until the mixture thickens.

Transfer the mixture to a warmed serving dish and sprinkle over the spring onions (scallions). Serve at once.

4 Servings

HUNG SHAO NGIU JOU
(Red-Cooked Beef with Star Anise)

	Metric/U.K.	U.S.
Vegetable oil	75ml/3floz	$\frac{3}{8}$ cup
Boned leg (shin) of beef, cubed	$1\frac{1}{2}$kg/3lb	3lb
Star anise	3 pieces	3 pieces
Water	150ml/5floz	$\frac{5}{8}$ cup
Beef stock cube, crumbled	$\frac{1}{2}$	$\frac{1}{2}$
Soy sauce	7 Tbs	7 Tbs
Fresh root ginger, peeled and finely chopped	4cm/$1\frac{1}{2}$in piece	$1\frac{1}{2}$in piece
Sugar	2 tsp	2 tsp
Red wine	150ml/5floz	$\frac{5}{8}$ cup

Preheat the oven to cool 150°C (Gas Mark 2, 300°F).

Heat the oil in a flameproof casserole. Add the beef cubes and fry until they are evenly browned. Remove from the heat and pour off all the excess oil. Stir in the star anise, water, stock cube and 4 tablespoons of soy sauce. Return the casserole to the heat and bring to the boil, stirring constantly. Transfer to the oven and cook for 1 hour, turning the meat once.

Remove from the oven and stir in the

remaining ingredients. Return to the oven and cook for a further 2 hours, turning the meat every 30 minutes.

Remove from the oven and serve at once.

6-8 Servings

QUICK-FRIED STEAK WITH VEGETABLES

The beef in this dish can either be cut with the grain into thin strips (the traditional Chinese way), or, simpler and probably more to the average western taste, the fillet steaks can simply be cut into two or three pieces, depending on their size.

	Metric/U.K.	U.S.
Sesame oil	50ml/2floz	¼ cup
Leek, separated into layers, then thinly sliced on the diagonal	1	1
Green pepper, pith and seeds removed and thinly sliced	1	1
Red pepper, pith and seeds removed and thinly sliced	1	1
Button mushrooms, sliced	50g/2oz	2oz
Bean sprouts	125g/4oz	4oz
Soy sauce	2 Tbs	2 Tbs
Hoi sin sauce	1 Tbs	1 Tbs
Fillet steaks, cut as above	½kg/1lb	1lb

Heat half the oil in a large frying-pan. Add the leek, peppers and mushrooms and stir-fry for 3 minutes. Add the bean sprouts, soy sauce and hoi sin sauce and stir-fry for a further 1 minute. Transfer the mixture to a warmed serving dish and keep hot while you cook the steak.

Add the remaining oil to the pan. When it is hot, add the steak pieces and either stir-fry (for strips) for 3 to 5 minutes, or until they are cooked through, or cook for 2 to 3 minutes on each side if they are steak pieces.

Arrange the steaks on top of the vegetables and serve at once.

2-3 Servings

SHAO K'O YANG JOU
(Steamed Lamb)

	Metric/U.K.	U.S.
Leg of lamb	1x1½kg/3lb	1x3lb
Crushed black peppercorns	1 tsp	1 tsp
Fresh root ginger, peeled and finely chopped	5cm/2in piece	2in piece
Mixed sweet pickle	125g/4oz	1 cup
Soy sauce	75ml/3floz	⅜ cup
Rice wine or dry sherry	150ml/5floz	⅝ cup
Onions, thinly sliced	2	2
Butter	1 tsp	1 tsp

Half-fill a saucepan with water and bring to the boil. Add the lamb, cover and boil for 4 minutes over moderately high heat. Remove from the heat and drain. Put the lamb on a chopping board and cut it, including the skin, into cubes. Arrange the cubes, skin side down, on the bottom of a heatproof basin. Sprinkle over the peppercorns and ginger and spoon over the pickle.

Combine the soy sauce and wine or sherry and pour over the meat. Arrange the onions on top. Cover with a circle of greaseproof or waxed paper about 10cm/4in wider than the rim of the basin and greased with butter. Cut out a circle of foil the same size, pleat the two and tie securely around the basin with string. Put the basin in a large saucepan and pour in enough boiling water to come about two-thirds of the way up the sides of the basin. Cover the pan and place over low heat. Steam for 2½ hours, adding more boiling water if necessary.

When the lamb has finished steaming, lift the basin out of the water and remove the foil and paper circles. Transfer the mixture to a warmed serving dish and serve at once.

6 Servings

QUICK-FRIED SPINACH WITH SHREDDED PORK

	Metric/U.K.	U.S.
Vegetable oil	3 Tbs	3 Tbs
Pork fillet (tenderloin), cut into thin strips	225g/8oz	8oz
Soy sauce	2 Tbs	2 Tbs

Quick-Fried Steak with Vegetables can either be cooked as in the picture in the western way, or the meat can be cut into strips with the grain and stir-fried in the Chinese way. Both are delicious.

	Metric/U.K.	U.S.
Rice wine or dry sherry	1 Tbs	1 Tbs
Sugar	1 tsp	1 tsp
Black pepper	½ tsp	½ tsp
Vegetable fat	40g/1½oz	3 Tbs
Spinach, trimmed and chopped	½kg/1lb	1lb
Salt	1 tsp	1 tsp

Heat the oil in a large saucepan. Add the pork strips and stir-fry for 2 minutes. Add the soy sauce, wine or sherry, sugar and pepper and stir-fry for a further 2 minutes. Using a slotted spoon, transfer the pork to a plate and keep hot.

Add 25g/1oz (2 tablespoons) of fat to the pan and melt it. Add the spinach and salt and stir-fry for 3 minutes. Add the remaining fat to the pan and stir-fry the mixture for a further 30 seconds. Using the slotted spoon, transfer the spinach to a warmed serving dish.

Increase the heat to moderately high and return the pork strips to the pan. Stir-fry for 30 seconds to reheat them thoroughly. Pour the pork and pan juices over the spinach and serve at once.

2 Servings

SWEET AND SOUR PORK

	Metric/U.K.	U.S.
Soy sauce	4 Tbs	4 Tbs
Fresh root ginger, peeled and grated	2½cm/1in piece	1in piece
Pork fillet (tenderloin), cubed	700g/1½lb	1½lb
Eggs	2	2
Cornflour (cornstarch)	3 Tbs	3 Tbs
Sufficient vegetable oil for deep-frying		
SAUCE		
Vegetable oil	2 Tbs	2 Tbs
Fresh root ginger, peeled and finely chopped	2½cm/1in piece	1in piece
Large carrots, thinly sliced on the diagonal	2	2
Large red pepper, pith and seeds removed and thinly sliced	1	1
Large green pepper, pith and seeds removed and thinly sliced	1	1
Canned pineapple chunks	450g/1lb	1lb
Soy sauce	1 Tbs	1 Tbs
Wine vinegar	3 Tbs	3 Tbs
Soft brown sugar	3 Tbs	3 Tbs
Salt	¼ tsp	¼ tsp
Cornflour (cornstarch), blended with 6 Tbs water	2 Tbs	2 Tbs

Combine the soy sauce and ginger together. Put the pork cubes in a bowl and pour over the soy sauce mixture. Baste the cubes to coat them thoroughly. Cover and set aside for 1 hour.

Mix the eggs and cornflour (cornstarch) together until they are smooth. Pour the batter over the pork cubes and mix well to blend.

Preheat the oven to moderate 180°C (Gas Mark 4, 350°F).

Fill a large saucepan one-third full with oil and heat until it reaches 185°C (360°F) on a deep-fat thermometer, or until a small cube of stale bread dropped into the oil turns golden in 50 seconds. Carefully lower the pork cubes, a few at a time, into the oil and fry for 5 to 6 minutes, or until they are golden brown and crisp. Transfer to an ovenproof dish as they cook and keep hot in the oven while you cook the remaining cubes, and make the sauce.

Heat the oil in a large frying-pan. Add the ginger, carrots and peppers and stir-fry for 3 minutes. Stir in the pineapple chunks with the can juice, the soy sauce, vinegar, sugar and salt and bring to the boil. Cook the sauce for 1 minute, stirring constantly. Stir in the cornflour (cornstarch) mixture until the sauce thickens and becomes translucent.

Remove the pork cubes from the oven. Pour over the sauce and serve at once.

4-6 Servings

LOU JO
(Pork Simmered in Master Sauce)

This dish, a speciality of Peking, is usually made with pork in China, but beef can be substituted if you prefer.

	Metric/U.K.	U.S.
Leg of pork, boned and trimmed of fat	1x1½kg/3lb	1x3lb

SAUCE

Soy sauce	600ml/1 pint	2½ cups
Rice wine or dry sherry	300ml/10floz	1¼ cups
Chicken stock	150ml/5floz	⅝ cup
Soft brown sugar	4 Tbs	4 Tbs
Garlic cloves, crushed	2	2
Fresh root ginger, peeled and sliced	2½cm/1in piece	1in piece
Bouquets garnis	2	2

Put the pork in a large saucepan and just cover with water. Bring to the boil, reduce the heat to moderate and cook for 6 minutes. Remove the pan from the heat, drain the pork and set

aside. Discard the cooking liquid.

To prepare the sauce, combine all the ingredients in a large saucepan. Bring to the boil, stirring frequently. Reduce the heat to low, arrange the pork in the sauce (making sure it is completely submerged), and simmer the mixture for 1½ hours, turning the pork every 30 minutes.

Remove from the heat and transfer the pork to a carving board. Cut into thin slices and arrange them decoratively on a serving dish. Strain the sauce into a sauceboat and pour a little over and around the meat. Serve at once, accompanied by the remaining sauce.

6-8 Servings

No book on Chinese cooking would be complete without Sweet and Sour Pork. In this particular version the pork cubes are deep-fried in batter and the sauce contains a colourful selection of vegetables and pineapple cubes.

SHAO JOU
(Cantonese Roast Pork)

This is one of the great classics of Cantonese cooking, often cooked (and badly) in the west. Hoi sin sauce is a rather spicy, sweet barbecue sauce available in cans or bottles from Chinese delicatessens.

	Metric/U.K.	U.S.
Pork fillet (tenderloin), cut into strips about 15cm/6in x 4cm/1½in	1½kg/3lb	3lb
Vegetable oil	2 Tbs	2 Tbs
MARINADE		
Medium onion, finely chopped	1	1
Soy sauce	5 Tbs	5 Tbs
Sugar	1 Tbs	1 Tbs
Rice wine or dry sherry	1 Tbs	1 Tbs
Ground ginger	1½ tsp	1½ tsp
Hoi sin sauce	1 Tbs	1 Tbs

To make the marinade, combine all the ingredients in a shallow dish. Add the pork strips and coat well. Set aside to marinate at room temperature for 2 hours, basting occasionally.

Preheat the oven to moderate 180°C (Gas Mark 4, 350°F).

Remove the pork from the marinade and reserve the marinade. Arrange the strips in a shallow roasting pan in one layer. Baste with half the reserved marinade and half the oil. Put the pan into the oven and roast the strips for 15 minutes. Remove from the oven and turn the strips over. Baste with the remaining marinade and remaining oil and return the pan to the oven. Roast the strips for a further 15 minutes.

Remove the pan from the oven and transfer the pork to a chopping board. Cut the strips into ½cm/¼in slices and serve at once.

8 Servings

RUN TSA LI CHI
(Plain Deep-Fried Sliced Pork)

	Metric/U.K.	U.S.
Pork fillets (tenderloin)	700g/1½lb	1½lb
Egg whites	2	2
Cornflour (cornstarch)	1½ Tbs	1½ Tbs
Sufficient vegetable oil for deep-frying		
DIP		
Black pepper	1 Tbs	1 Tbs
Salt	1 Tbs	1 Tbs

Slice the pork against the grain into thin slices. Using a mallet, beat the slices until they are very thin, then cut into strips about 7½cm/3in by 5cm/2in. Put the strips into a large bowl and set aside.

Beat the egg whites until they are frothy. Gradually beat in the cornflour (cornstarch) until the mixture forms a smooth batter. Pour the batter over the pork strips and toss to coat thoroughly. Set aside for 10 minutes.

Fill a large saucepan one-third full with oil and heat until it reaches 185°C (360°F) on a deep-fat thermometer, or until a small cube of stale bread dropped into the oil turns golden in 50 seconds. Carefully lower the meat strips, a few at a time, into the oil and cook for 1 minute or until they are golden brown and crisp. Remove from the oil and drain on kitchen towels.

To make the dip, fry the pepper and salt in a small frying-pan over moderately high heat for 4 minutes, stirring constantly. Remove from the heat and transfer the mixture to a small serving bowl.

Serve the pork strips at once, with the dip.

4-6 Servings

CHINESE ROAST PORK

This dish can be eaten either hot or cold and is traditionally accompanied by Chinese mustard.

	Metric/U.K.	U.S.
Loin of pork, boned and trimmed of fat	1x1½kg/3lb	1x3lb
Soy sauce	50ml/2floz	¼ cup
Soft brown sugar	4 Tbs	4 Tbs
Salt and pepper to taste		
Rice wine or dry sherry	2 Tbs	2 Tbs
Fresh root ginger, peeled and sliced	2½cm/1in piece	1in piece

Cut the meat in half. Combine the soy sauce, sugar, salt, pepper, wine or sherry and ginger in a large dish. Add the pork and marinate at

Shao Jou or Roast Pork is one of the classics of Cantonese cooking.

Ching-Chiao-Chao Jiu-Jou (steak with pepper—recipe on page 23) and Chinese Roast Pork make a delightful meal served, as here, with fried rice.

room temperature for 4 hours, basting frequently.

Preheat the oven to fairly hot 190°C (Gas Mark 5, 375°F). Put the pork and marinade in a roasting pan and roast for 10 minutes. Turn the meat over and increase the temperature to very hot 230°C (Gas Mark 8, 450°F). Continue to roast for about 40 minutes, turning and basting frequently during cooking, or until the pork is cooked through and tender.

Preheat the grill (broiler) to high.

Put the meat under the grill (broiler) and grill (broil) for 4 to 6 minutes, or until the meat is evenly browned.

Transfer to a serving dish, discarding the marinade, and cut into slices before serving.

6 Servings

KUO PA JOU TIN
(Diced Pork on Crackling Rice)

The English translation of this dish describes the sound the rice is supposed to make when the pork sauce is poured over it.

	Metric/U.K.	U.S.
Pork fillet (tenderloin), cubed	½kg/1lb	1lb
Salt and pepper to taste		
Cornflour (cornstarch)	1½ Tbs	1½ Tbs
Cooked long-grain rice	450g/1lb	6 cups
Sufficient vegetable oil for deep-frying		

SAUCE		
Chicken stock	150ml/5floz	$\frac{5}{8}$ cup
Soy sauce	3 Tbs	3 Tbs
Sugar	1 Tbs	1 Tbs
Rice wine or dry sherry	2 Tbs	2 Tbs
Corn oil	2 Tbs	2 Tbs
Onion, thinly sliced	1	1
Garlic clove, crushed	1	1
Cornflour (cornstarch), blended with 4 Tbs water	1$\frac{1}{2}$ Tbs	1$\frac{1}{2}$ Tbs

Preheat the oven to very cool 140°C (Gas Mark 1, 275°F).

Sprinkle the pork cubes with salt, pepper and cornflour (cornstarch), rubbing them into the meat with your fingers.

Put the rice into an ovenproof baking dish and put the dish into the oven. Dry out the rice for 15 to 20 minutes, or until it is slightly crisp.

Meanwhile, fill a large saucepan one-third full with oil and heat until it reaches 185°C (360°F) on a deep-fat thermometer, or until a small cube of stale bread dropped into the oil turns golden brown in 50 seconds. Carefully lower the pork cubes, a few at a time, into the oil and fry for 3 to 4 minutes, or until they are golden brown and crisp. Remove from the oil and drain on kitchen towels.

To prepare the sauce, combine the stock, soy sauce, sugar and wine or sherry.

Heat the corn oil in a large frying-pan. Add the onion and garlic and stir-fry for 1 minute. Pour over the stock mixture and bring to the boil. Add the pork cubes, basting well, and reduce the heat to low. Simmer the mixture for 2 minutes. Stir in the cornflour (cornstarch) mixture and cook until the sauce has thickened and become translucent. Set aside and keep hot.

Remove the rice from the oven.

Return the saucepan with the oil to moderate heat and reheat the oil until it reaches 180°C (350°F) on a deep-fat thermometer, or until a small cube of stale bread dropped into the oil turns golden in 55 seconds. Put the rice in a narrow-meshed deep-frying basket and carefully lower it into the oil. Cook the rice for 1$\frac{1}{2}$ minutes, then remove from the oil and drain on kitchen towels.

Arrange the rice on a warmed serving dish and pour over the pork sauce.

Serve at once.

4 Servings

MEE FENG JOU
(Pork in Ground Rice)

This delicious dish is traditionally served with a variety of dips such as tomato-soy sauce (mix together equal quantities of tomato ketchup and soy sauce), garlic-soy (finely chop 3 garlic cloves and mix with 4 tablespoons of soy sauce) and soy-sherry-chilli (3 tablespoons each of soy sauce and sherry with 1 tablespoon of chilli sauce).

	Metric/U.K.	U.K.
Leg or belly of pork	1kg/2lb	2lb
Fresh root ginger, peeled and finely chopped	4cm/1$\frac{1}{2}$in piece	1$\frac{1}{2}$in piece
Soy sauce	2 Tbs	2 Tbs
Chilli sauce	1$\frac{1}{2}$ tsp	1$\frac{1}{2}$ tsp
Coarsely ground rice	150g/5oz	1$\frac{1}{4}$ cups

Cut the pork into 7$\frac{1}{2}$cm/3in by 4cm/1$\frac{1}{2}$in slices, about $\frac{1}{2}$cm/$\frac{1}{4}$in thick.

Mix together the ginger, soy sauce and chilli sauce and rub the mixture over the pork slices so that they are evenly coated on both sides. Set aside to marinate for 1 hour.

Heat a large frying-pan over moderate heat. Add the rice to the pan and cook, stirring constantly, until it begins to brown. Put the pork pieces in the pan and turn them so that they become thickly coated with the rice. Remove from the heat.

Transfer the pork pieces to a heatproof dish, arranging them in 'tile-piece' or 'fish-scale' fashion. Place the dish in a steamer, cover and steam over moderate heat for 35 to 40 minutes, or until the pork is cooked through and tender.

Remove the dish from the steamer and serve the pork, with the dips.

4-6 Servings

JOU SI CHOW CHING TS'AI
Shredded Pork Stir-Fried with Spring Greens)

	Metric/U.K.	U.S.
Lean pork, cut into thin strips	350g/12oz	12oz
Salt and pepper to taste		
Cornflour (cornstarch)	2 tsp	2 tsp
Vegetable oil	3 Tbs	3 Tbs
Spring greens or		

	Metric/U.K.	U.S.
cabbage, shredded	½kg/1lb	1lb
Vegetable fat	15g/½oz	1 Tbs
Beef stock	50ml/2floz	4 Tbs
Soy sauce	2 Tbs	2 Tbs
Sugar	1 tsp	1 tsp
Rice wine or dry sherry	2 Tbs	2 Tbs

Put the pork strips on a plate and sprinkle them with salt, pepper and cornflour (cornstarch), rubbing them into the meat with your fingers.

Heat the oil in a large frying-pan. Add the pork and stir-fry over high heat for 3 minutes. Push the pork to the side of the pan and add the greens or cabbage and vegetable fat. Mix the greens or cabbage with the remainder of the oil and the fat. Reduce the heat to moderate and stir in the stock, soy sauce and sugar. Fry the greens or cabbage, turning constantly, for 3 minutes.

Stir the pork strips into the vegetables, mixing until they are well blended. Pour the wine or sherry over the mixture and stir-fry for a further 1 minute.

Remove from the heat and transfer the mixture to a warm serving dish. Serve at once.

4 Servings

JOU YUAN TS'A HUI
(Meatball Chop Suey)

	Metric/U.K.	U.S.
Lean pork, minced (ground)	350g/12oz	12oz
Canned water chestnuts, drained and chopped	50g/2oz	2oz
Small egg	1	1
Sugar	½ tsp	½ tsp
Salt and white pepper to taste		
Soy sauce	1 Tbs	1 Tbs
Cornflour (cornstarch)	1 Tbs	1 Tbs
Sufficient vegetable oil for deep-frying		
Peanut oil	2 Tbs	2 Tbs
Medium onions, thinly sliced	2	2
Cabbage, shredded	225g/8oz	8oz
Chicken stock	300ml/10floz	1¼ cups
Bean sprouts	225g/8oz	8oz

	Metric/U.K.	U.S.
Small cucumber, shredded lengthways	¼	¼

Combine the pork, water chestnuts, egg, sugar, seasoning, soy sauce and cornflour (cornstarch) until they are smooth. Form the mixture into 10 or 12 small balls and set aside.

Fill a large saucepan one-third full with oil and heat until it reaches 185°C (360°F) on a deep-fat thermometer, or until a small cube of stale bread dropped into the oil turns golden in 50 seconds. Arrange a few of the meatballs in a deep-frying basket and carefully lower them into the oil. Fry for 3 to 4 minutes, or until they are lightly browned and crisp. Remove from the pan and drain on kitchen towels. Keep hot while you fry the remaining meatballs in the same way.

Heat the 2 tablespoons of oil in a flameproof casserole. Add the onions and cabbage and fry until they are soft. Pour in the stock and bring to the boil. Reduce the heat to low and simmer the mixture for 15 minutes, stirring occasionally. Spread the bean sprouts over the cabbage mixture, then top with the shredded cucumber. Arrange the meatballs on top of the vegetables. Simmer the mixture for 8 minutes. Serve at once.

4 Servings

YU HSIANG JOU SI
(Quick-Fried Pork with 'Fish' Ingredients)

	Metric/U.K.	U.S.
Pork fillet (tenderloin), thinly sliced then shredded	½kg/1lb	1lb
Soy sauce	4 Tbs	4 Tbs
Cornflour (cornstarch), blended with 2 Tbs water	2 tsp	2 tsp
Vegetable oil	5 Tbs	5 Tbs
Dried salted black beans, soaked in cold water for 15 minutes, drained and chopped	2 Tbs	2 Tbs
Small dried chillis, finely chopped	2	2
Garlic cloves, crushed	2	2
Chinese dried mushrooms, soaked in cold water for 20 minutes, drained and		

Yu-Lang-Chi (chicken and ham with broccoli—recipe on page 41) and Yu Hsiang Jou Si (quick-fried pork with 'fish' ingredients). The latter is one of the specialities of the province of Szechuan, where meat is often cooked with ingredients more commonly associated with fish or shellfish—hence the translation of the title.

	Metric/U.K.	U.S.
finely chopped	4	4
Leek, white part only, finely chopped	1	1
'Wood ear' fungi	1 Tbs	1 Tbs
Fresh root ginger, peeled and finely chopped	2½cm/1in piece	1in piece
Canned bamboo shoot, drained and chopped	75g/3oz	3oz
Sesame oil	2 tsp	2 tsp
Wine vinegar	1½ Tbs	1½ Tbs
Rice wine or dry sherry	2 Tbs	2 Tbs
Sugar	1½ tsp	1½ tsp

Combine the pork and 2 tablespoons of soy sauce. Work the sauce into the meat with your fingers. Add the cornflour (cornstarch) mixture and stir to blend. Set aside for 10 minutes.

Heat 3 tablespoons of oil in a frying-pan. When it is hot, add the pork mixture, spreading it out over the bottom of the pan. Stir-fry for 1 minute. Using a slotted spoon, transfer the pork strips to a plate.

Add the remaining oil to the pan. Add the black beans and chillis and stir-fry for 10 seconds. Increase the heat to moderately high and add the garlic, vegetables, ginger and bamboo shoot. Stir-fry for 3 minutes. Return the pork to the pan and stir in the sesame oil, remaining soy sauce, vinegar, wine or sherry and sugar. Stir-fry for 1½ minutes, or until the mixture is heated through.

Transfer the mixture to a warmed serving dish and serve at once.

4 Servings

PORK WITH MIXED VEGETABLES

	Metric/U.K.	U.S.
Pork fillet (tenderoin),		

cut into thin strips		
5cm/2in x ½cm/¼in	700g/1½lb	1½lb
Vegetable oil	5 Tbs	5 Tbs
Chinese dried mushrooms, soaked in cold water for 20 minutes, drained and sliced	10	10
sliced onion	1	1
Celery stalks, cut into thin strips	2	2
Green pepper, pith and seeds removed and cut into thin strips	1	1
Canned water chestnuts, drained and sliced	10	10
Bean sprouts	½kg/1lb	1lb
Salt	1 tsp	1 tsp
Sugar	1 tsp	1 tsp
Soy sauce	2 Tbs	2 Tbs
Rice wine or dry sherry	2 Tbs	2 Tbs
MARINADE		
Soy sauce	2 Tbs	2 Tbs
Fresh root ginger, peeled and finely chopped	2½cm/1in piece	1in piece
Salt	1 tsp	1 tsp
Monosodium glutamate (MSG), (optional)	¼ tsp	¼ tsp
Sugar	2 tsp	2 tsp
Garlic cloves, crushed	2	2
Rice wine or dry sherry	2 Tbs	2 Tbs

To make the marinade, combine all the ingredients in a large bowl. Add the pork strips and stir until the meat is thoroughly coated. Set aside to marinate for 30 minutes.

Heat 2 tablespoons of oil in a large deep frying-pan. Add the mushrooms, onion, celery, pepper and water chestnuts, and stir-fry for 2 minutes. Using a slotted spoon, transfer the vegetables to a plate and keep hot.

Add the remaining oil to the pan. Add the pork slices and marinade and stir-fry for 5 minutes, or until the pork is deeply and evenly browned. Stir in the reserved vegetables and bean sprouts, then the salt, sugar, soy sauce and wine or sherry. Stir-fry for a further 3 minutes.

Transfer the mixture to a warmed serving dish and serve at once.

4-6 Servings

Pork with Mixed Vegetables is a filling yet inexpensive dish.

MI TSE HO-TUI
(Ham in Honey Syrup)

	Metric/U.K.	U.S.
Middle leg of gammon (ham), soaked overnight in cold water and drained	1x1½kg/3lb	1x3lb
SAUCE		
Sugar	2 Tbs	2 Tbs
Water	4 Tbs	4 Tbs
Clear honey	2 Tbs	2 Tbs
Rice wine or dry sherry	2 Tbs	2 Tbs
Cherry brandy	2 tsp	2 tsp
Cornflour (cornstarch) blended with 3 Tbs water	2 tsp	2 tsp

Half-fill the lower part of a large steamer with boiling water. Put the gammon (ham) in the upper part and place the steamer over moderate heat. Steam the gammon (ham) for 2¼ hours. Remove the steamer from the heat and set the gammon (ham) aside until it is cool enough to handle. When it is cool enough to handle, cut it into ½cm/¼in thick slices. Arrange the slices decoratively on a heatproof serving dish.

To make the sauce, combine all the sauce ingredients in a small saucepan and bring to the boil, stirring constantly. Remove from the heat and pour over the ham slices. Put the serving dish in the top part of the steamer and return the steamer to moderate heat. Steam the meat and sauce for 5 minutes.

Remove the steamer from the heat and carefully remove the dish from the steamer. Serve at once.

6-8 Servings

DEEP-FRIED SWEETBREADS

	Metric/U.K.	U.S.
Sweetbreads, soaked in cold water for 3 hours, drained, skinned and trimmed	1kg/2lb	2lb
Eggs, lightly beaten	2	2
Seasoned cornflour (cornstarch), made with cornflour (cornstarch), salt, pepper and ground ginger to taste	50g/2oz	½ cup
Sufficient vegetable oil for deep-frying		
SAUCE		
Vegetable oil	2 Tbs	2 Tbs
Small onion, finely chopped	1	1
Fresh root ginger, peeled and finely chopped	5cm/2in piece	2in piece
Large green peppers, pith and seeds removed and chopped	2	2
Garlic cloves, chopped	2	2
French (green) beans, cut into 5cm/2in lengths	125g/4oz	4oz
Bean sprouts	125g/4oz	4oz
Canned pineapple chunks	450g/1lb	1lb
Soy sauce	2 Tbs	2 Tbs
White wine vinegar	4 Tbs	4 Tbs
Soft brown sugar	4 Tbs	4 Tbs
Salt	¼ tsp	¼ tsp
Cornflour (cornstarch), blended with 6 Tbs water	2 Tbs	2 Tbs

Put the sweetbreads in a large saucepan and just cover with water. Bring to the boil, remove the pan from the heat and set aside for 10 minutes. Remove the sweetbreads from the

pan and drain on kitchen towels. Discard the water. Cut the sweetbreads into 1cm/½in slices and transfer them to a bowl.

Beat the eggs and seasoned cornflour (cornstarch) together until they form a smooth batter. Pour the batter over the sweetbreads and toss gently to coat them thoroughly. Set

aside for 10 minutes.

Preheat the oven to cool 150°C (Gas Mark 2, 300°F).

Fill a large saucepan one-third full with oil and heat until it reaches 185°C (360°F) on a deep-fat thermometer, or until a small cube of stale bread dropped into the oil turns golden in

Sweet and Sour Liver—a new way to serve a traditional and nutritious meat. The sauce contains orange juice which blends beautifully with the richness of the liver.

50 seconds. Carefully lower the sweetbread slices into the oil, a few at a time, and fry for 5 to 6 minutes, or until they are golden brown and crisp. Remove the slices from the oil and drain on kitchen towels. Transfer the slices to an ovenproof dish, cover and put the dish into the oven to keep warm while you make the sauce.

Heat the oil in a large frying-pan. Add the onion, ginger, peppers, garlic and beans and fry until they are soft. Stir in the bean sprouts, pineapple chunks and can juice, the soy sauce, vinegar, sugar and salt, and bring to the boil. Cook for 1 minute, stirring constantly. Stir in the cornflour (cornstarch) mixture and cook, stirring constantly, until the sauce thickens and becomes translucent. Remove the pan from the heat.

Remove the sweetbreads from the oven and pour over the sauce.

Serve at once.

6-8 Servings

SWEET AND SOUR LIVER

	Metric/U.K.	U.S.
Lambs' liver, cut into 7½cm/3in x 5cm/2in pieces	700g/1½lb	1½lb
Sufficient vegetable oil for deep-frying		
MARINADE		
Soy sauce	5 Tbs	5 Tbs
Rice wine or dry sherry	2 Tbs	2 Tbs
Sugar	2 tsp	2 tsp
SAUCE		
Wine vinegar	4 Tbs	4 Tbs
Sugar	3 Tbs	3 Tbs
Orange juice	3 Tbs	3 Tbs
Tomato purée (paste)	1 Tbs	1 Tbs
Soy sauce	1½ Tbs	1½ Tbs
Rice wine or dry sherry	1½ Tbs	1½ Tbs

	Metric/U.K.	U.S.
Cornflour (cornstarch), blended with 5 Tbs water	1 Tbs	1 Tbs

Combine all the marinade ingredients in a large shallow bowl. Add the liver pieces and baste well. Set aside at room temperature for 3 hours, basting occasionally. Remove from the marinade and pat dry with kitchen towels. Discard the marinade.

Fill a large saucepan one-third full with oil and heat until it reaches 185°C (360°F) on a deep-fat thermometer, or until a small cube of stale bread dropped into the oil turns golden in 50 seconds. Carefully lower the liver pieces into the oil, a few at a time, and fry for 1 minute or until they are brown and crisp. Remove from the oil and drain on kitchen towels.

Combine all the sauce ingredients in a large saucepan and bring to the boil, stirring constantly. Add the liver pieces to the sauce and cook, stirring constantly, until the sauce thickens and becomes translucent.

Transfer the mixture to a warmed serving dish and serve at once.

6 Servings

RUN TSA CHIN KAN
(Deep-Fried Liver and Kidneys)

	Metric/U.K.	U.S.
Lambs' liver	350g/12oz	12oz
Lambs' kidneys, prepared	350g/12oz	12oz
Soy sauce	5 Tbs	5 Tbs
Rice wine or dry sherry	2 Tbs	2 Tbs
Sugar	2 tsp	2 tsp
Sufficient vegetable oil for deep-frying		
DIP		
Black pepper	1 Tbs	1 Tbs
Salt	1 Tbs	1 Tbs

Slice the liver and kidneys thinly, then cut into thin strips about 4cm/1½in by 2½cm/1in. Put the liver strips in one bowl and the kidney strips in another.

Combine the soy sauce, wine or sherry and sugar, then pour equal quantities of the mixture over the liver and kidneys, gently tossing the strips to coat them thoroughly. Set aside to marinate at room temperature for 3 hours, basting occasionally.

Fill a large saucepan one-third full with oil and heat until it reaches 185°C (360°F) on a deep-fat thermometer, or until a small cube of stale bread dropped into the oil turns golden brown in 50 seconds. Carefully lower the liver strips into the oil and cook for 1 minute or until they are brown and crisp. Remove from the oil and drain on kitchen towels. Keep hot while you fry the kidney strips in the same way.

To make the dip, fry the pepper and salt in a small frying-pan over moderately high heat for 4 minutes, stirring constantly. Remove from the heat and transfer the mixture to a small serving bowl.

Serve the liver and kidney strips at once, accompanied by the dip.

4-6 Servings

LIN-MOUN CHI
(Lemon Chicken)

	Metric/U.K.	U.S.
Chicken, skinned	1x1½kg/3lb	1x3lb
Salt	1½ tsp	1½ tsp
Ground ginger	1 tsp	1 tsp
Egg, lightly beaten	1	1
Ground rice	125g/4oz	1 cup
Sufficient vegetable oil for deep-frying		
Juice of 1 lemon		
Chopped spring onions (scallions)	1 Tbs	1 Tbs
Lemon, cut into thin slices	1	1
SAUCE Chicken stock	50ml/2floz	¼ cup
Rice wine or dry sherry	2 Tbs	2 Tbs
Salt	¼ tsp	¼ tsp
Sugar	1 tsp	1 tsp

Cut the chicken through the bone, into 16 or 20 pieces. Sprinkle the pieces with salt and ginger, rubbing them into the flesh. Put the egg in a saucer and dip the chicken pieces in it, one by one, then roll in the ground rice until they are thoroughly coated.

Fill a large saucepan one-third full with oil and heat until it reaches 185°C (360°F) on a deep-fat thermometer, or until a small cube of

stale bread dropped into the oil turns golden in 50 seconds. Put a few of the chicken pieces in a deep-frying basket and carefully lower the basket into the oil. Fry for 3 to 5 minutes, or until the pieces are golden brown and crisp. Remove from the oil and drain on kitchen towels.

To make the sauce, put all the ingredients in a small saucepan and bring to the boil. Remove from the heat and pour over the chicken pieces.

Sprinkle the lemon juice and spring onions (scallions) over the chicken. Arrange the lemon slices around the chicken and serve at once.

4-6 Servings

KUO TIEH CHI
(Egg-Braised Chicken)

	Metric/U.K.	U.S.
Boned chicken breasts, cut into thin strips about 5cm/2in x 2½cm/1in	350g/12oz	12oz
Salt and pepper to taste		
Sugar	2 tsp	2 tsp
Chilli sauce	1 tsp	1 tsp
Dry white wine	2 Tbs	2 Tbs
Cornflour (cornstarch)	1 Tbs	1 Tbs
Sufficient vegetable oil for deep-frying		
Eggs, lightly beaten	3	3
Sesame oil	75ml/3floz	⅜ cup
Chopped parsley	1 Tbs	1 Tbs
Rice wine or dry sherry	1½ Tbs	1½ Tbs
Soy sauce	1½ Tbs	1½ Tbs
Lemon juice	1½ Tbs	1½ Tbs

Sprinkle the chicken strips with the salt, pepper, sugar, chilli sauce, wine and cornflour (cornstarch), rubbing them into the meat with your fingers. Set aside to marinate at room temperature for 1½ hours.

Fill a large saucepan one-third full with oil and heat until it reaches 185°C (360°F) on a deep-fat thermometer, or until a small cube of stale bread dropped into the oil turns golden in 50 seconds. Carefully lower the chicken strips, a few at a time, into the oil and fry for 1 to 2 minutes, or until they are golden brown. Remove from the oil and drain on kitchen towels.

Put the eggs into a shallow bowl. When the chicken strips have been cooked, dip the strips, one by one, into the eggs and coat thickly.

Heat the sesame oil in a frying-pan. Add the chicken strips to the pan, in one layer if possible, and shake and tilt gently to distribute the oil evenly. Fry the strips, turning occasionally, for 2 minutes.

Remove the strips from the pan and arrange them, in one layer, on a very large, warmed serving dish. Sprinkle with the parsley, wine or sherry, soy sauce and lemon juice, and serve at once.

4 Servings

YU-LANG-CHI
(Chicken and Ham)

	Metric/U.K.	U.S.
Chicken stock	1¾l/3 pints	7½ cups
Fresh root ginger, peeled and sliced	2½cm/1in piece	1in piece
Spring onions (scallions), cut into 5cm/2in lengths	2	2
Chicken	1x2kg/4lb	1x4lb
Parma ham, cut into strips	4 slices	4 slices
Broccoli, broken into flowerets	1kg/2lb	2lb
Soy sauce	2 tsp	2 tsp
Cornflour (cornstarch), blended with 1 Tbs water	1 tsp	1 tsp

Put the stock, ginger and spring onions (scallions) into a saucepan and bring to the boil. Add the chicken, and add more boiling water to cover the chicken if necessary. Bring to the boil again. Reduce the heat to low, cover and simmer for 30 minutes. Remove from the heat and set aside for 2 hours. (During this time it will cook through.)

Transfer the chicken to a chopping board. Remove the flesh from the bones, discarding the skin, and cut into serving pieces. Arrange the chicken pieces and ham on a warmed dish. Keep hot.

Pour off and discard all but 450ml/15floz (2 cups) of stock. Strain and return it to the pan and bring to the boil. Add the broccoli and return to the boil. Remove the pan from the

Kuo Pa Jou Tin (diced pork on crackling rice—recipe page 30) is a favourite method of cooking in China. Kuo Tieh Chi (egg-braised chicken) is an unusual and satisfying dish where chicken strips are twice cooked, once by deep frying, once by shallow frying in an egg batter.

heat and soak the broccoli in the stock for 5 minutes.

Drain the broccoli, reserving 125ml/4floz (½ cup) of stock. Arrange the broccoli around the chicken and ham, and keep hot.

Combine the soy sauce and reserved stock in a saucepan and bring to the boil. Add the cornflour (cornstarch) mixture and, when the liquid thickens slightly, remove the pan from the heat. Pour over the chicken and ham and serve.

4-6 Servings

QUICK-FRIED CHICKEN CUBES IN WHITE SAUCE

	Metric/U.K.	U.S.
Chicken breasts, boned	4	4
Ground ginger	¼ tsp	¼ tsp
Salt and pepper to taste		
Cornflour (cornstarch)	1 Tbs	1 Tbs
Butter	1 Tbs	1 Tbs
Vegetable oil	2 Tbs	2 Tbs
Small shelled shrimps	125g/4oz	4oz
Small red pepper, pith and seeds removed and cut into 1cm/½in lengths	1	1
Cucumber, halved and cut into 1cm/½in lengths	¼	¼
SAUCE Chicken stock	75ml/3floz	⅜ cup
Butter	1 Tbs	1 Tbs
Dry white wine	50ml/2floz	¼ cup
Cornflour (cornstarch), blended with 4 Tbs water	1 Tbs	1 Tbs
Single (light) cream	125ml/4floz	½ cup

Cut the chicken breasts into small cubes and rub them with ginger, seasoning and cornflour (cornstarch).

Melt the butter with the oil in a large frying-pan. Add the chicken cubes and stir-fry for 30 seconds. Add the shrimps, pepper and cucumber to the pan and stir-fry the mixture for 2 minutes. Remove from the heat.

To make the sauce, pour the stock into a small saucepan and bring to the boil. Stir in the butter and wine and cook until the butter has melted. Reduce the heat to low and add the cornflour (cornstarch) mixture, stirring constantly. Simmer for 2 minutes, or until the sauce has thickened. Stir in the cream. Remove from the heat and pour the sauce into the frying-pan. Return the pan to moderate heat and cook, turning the meat and vegetables over in the sauce, for 2 minutes.

Transfer the mixture to a warmed serving dish and serve at once.

4 Servings

HUNG SHAO CHI
(Red-Cooked Chicken)

The chicken suggested for this recipe is a roasting one, but if you wish to economize and use a boiling chicken, increase the cooking time by 40 minutes.

	Metric/U.K.	U.S.
Spring onions (scallions), cut into 5cm/2in lengths	2	2
Fresh root ginger, peeled and chopped	4cm/1½in piece	1½in piece
Oven-ready chicken	1x1½kg/3lb	1x3lb
Vegetable oil	75ml/3floz	⅜ cup
Soy sauce	75ml/3floz	⅜ cup
Water	300ml/10floz	1¼ cups
Chicken stock cube, crumbled	½	½
Sugar	2 tsp	2 tsp
Rice wine or dry sherry	3 Tbs	3 Tbs

Stuff the spring onions (scallions) and ginger into the cavity of the chicken and secure with a skewer or trussing needle and thread.

Heat the oil in a large saucepan. Add the chicken and fry until it is lightly browned all over. Remove the pan from the heat and pour off all the excess oil. Add the soy sauce, water, stock cube, sugar and wine or sherry. Return to the heat and bring to the boil, stirring occasionally. Reduce the heat to low, cover the pan and simmer for 30 minutes. Turn the chicken over and re-cover. Simmer for a further 45 minutes, or until the chicken is cooked through and tender.

Transfer the chicken to a carving board. Untruss and carve into serving pieces. Transfer the pieces to a warmed serving dish. Pour over the cooking liquid and serve at once.

4-6 Servings

Two very different but very tasty quick-fry dishes—on the left Quick-Fried Spinach with Shredded Pork (recipe page 25) and on the right Quick-Fried Chicken Cubes in White Sauce.

HO TAO CHI TIN
(Quick-Fried Chicken Cubes with Walnuts)

	Metric/U.K.	U.S.
Chicken breasts, boned	½kg/1lb	1lb
Salt	1 tsp	1 tsp
Cornflour (cornstarch)	1 Tbs	1 Tbs
Egg white, lightly beaten	1	1
Vegetable oil	75ml/3floz	⅜ cup
Shelled walnuts, halved	225g/8oz	2 cups
Sugar	1 tsp	1 tsp
Soy sauce	1 Tbs	1 Tbs
Rice wine or dry sherry	2 Tbs	2 Tbs

Cut the chicken flesh into bite-sized pieces. Mix the salt and cornflour (cornstarch) together, then rub into the chicken pieces. Put the cubes in a bowl and pour over the egg white. Toss gently to coat the cubes thoroughly.

Heat the oil in a large frying-pan. Add the chicken cubes and stir-fry over high heat for

2 minutes. Using a slotted spoon, transfer the cubes to a plate and set aside. Pour off all but 1 tablespoon of oil from the pan and add the walnuts. Reduce the heat to moderate and stir-fry the walnuts for 1 minute. Return the chicken cubes to the pan and stir-fry for a further 1 minute.

Sprinkle over the remaining ingredients and stir-fry for 1½ minutes. Transfer the mixture to a warmed serving dish and serve at once.

4 Servings

PAI CHIU TUNG CHI
(Long-Simmered Chicken in White Wine)

The cooking liquid from this delicious dish is often served as a separate soup course.

	Metric/U.K.	U.S.
Chicken, cleaned	1 x 1¾kg/3½lb	1 x 3½lb
Water	600ml/1 pint	2½ cups
Dry white wine	300ml/10floz	1¼ cups
Soy sauce	3 Tbs	3 Tbs
Sesame oil	1½ Tbs	1½ Tbs
Chinese cabbage, shredded	½kg/1lb	1lb
STUFFING		
Long-grain rice, soaked in cold water for 30 minutes and drained	75g/3oz	½ cup
Spring onions (scallions), chopped	4	4
Lean bacon, chopped	4 slices	4 slices
Fresh root ginger, peeled and chopped	5cm/2in piece	2in piece
Chicken stock cube, crumbled	1	1
Salt and pepper to taste		

Preheat the oven to cool 150°C (Gas Mark 2, 300°F).

To make the stuffing, combine all the ingredients together then stuff into the cavity of the chicken. Close with a skewer or a trussing needle and thread. Put the chicken into a flameproof casserole and pour over the water. Bring to the boil, then transfer the casserole to the oven and bake for 1 hour.

Add the wine to the casserole and cook the chicken for a further 45 minutes, or until it is cooked through and tender. Transfer the chicken to a warmed serving dish and keep hot.

Combine the soy sauce and sesame oil in a small bowl, then pour over the chicken and serve at once. If you wish to serve the cooking liquid as a soup course, stir in the cabbage and put the casserole over moderate heat. Cook for 5 minutes, remove from the heat and serve at once.

4-6 Servings

PAI CHOU CHI
(White Cooked Chicken)

	Metric/U.K.	U.S.
Water	2½l/4 pints	5 pints
Chicken, cleaned	1x1½kg/3lb	1x3lb
Spring onions (scallions), finely chopped	5	5
SAUCE A		
Fresh root ginger, peeled and finely chopped	5cm/2in piece	2in piece
Boiling water	5 Tbs	5 Tbs
Hot oil	1 Tbs	1 Tbs
Salt	½ tsp	½ tsp
SAUCE B		
Garlic cloves, crushed	2	2
Soy sauce	3 Tbs	3 Tbs
Vinegar	2 Tbs	2 Tbs

Bring the water to the boil in a large saucepan. Add the chicken and return to the boil. Reduce the heat to low and simmer for 1 hour. Remove from the heat, cover and leave the chicken for 3 hours.

Drain the chicken and discard the cooking liquid. Transfer the chicken to a chopping board and cut, through the bone, into about 20 large-bite pieces. Transfer to a serving plate and set aside.

To make sauce A, put the ginger in a small serving bowl. Add the remaining ingredients and stir to blend.

To make sauce B, put the garlic in a small serving bowl. Add the soy sauce and vinegar and stir to blend.

Sprinkle the chopped spring onions (scallions) over the chicken pieces and serve, with the sauces.

4-6 Servings

SWEET AND SOUR CHICKEN

	Metric/U.K.	U.S.
Chicken breasts, skinned	4	4
Salt and pepper to taste		
Ground ginger	1 tsp	1 tsp
Egg whites, lightly beaten	2	2
Cornflour (cornstarch)	2 Tbs	2 Tbs
Sufficient vegetable oil for deep-frying		
SAUCE		
Vegetable oil	50ml/2floz	¼ cup
Fresh root ginger, peeled and chopped	5cm/2in piece	2in piece
Large green pepper, pith and seeds removed and chopped	1	1
Cucumber, halved lengthways and sliced	½	½
Spring onions (scallions), finely chopped	5	5
Bean sprouts	175g/6oz	6oz
Canned pineapple chunks	225g/8oz	8oz
Wine vinegar	4 Tbs	4 Tbs
Soy sauce	1½ Tbs	1½ Tbs
Tomato purée (paste)	2 Tbs	2 Tbs
Soft brown sugar	2 Tbs	2 Tbs
Cornflour (cornstarch), blended with 3 Tbs water	1 Tbs	1 Tbs

Cut the chicken breasts into bite-sized pieces and rub the flesh with salt, pepper and ground ginger. Put the pieces into a shallow dish. Beat the egg whites and cornflour (cornstarch) together, then pour the mixture over the chicken pieces, tossing gently until they are thoroughly coated. Set aside for 15 minutes, basting occasionally.

Preheat the oven to warm 150°C (Gas Mark 2, 300°F).

Fill a large saucepan one-third full with oil and heat until it reaches 180°C (350°F) on a deep-fat thermometer, or until a small cube of stale bread dropped into the oil turns golden in 55 seconds. Carefully lower the chicken cubes, a few at a time, into the oil and fry for 3 to 4 minutes, or until they are lightly browned and crisp. Remove from the oil and drain on kitchen towels. Transfer the cubes to a serving dish and keep hot in the oven while you cook the sauce.

Heat the oil in a very large frying-pan. Add the ginger and stir-fry for 30 seconds. Add the vegetables and pineapple chunks and stir-fry for 3 minutes. Combine the pineapple can juice and the remaining ingredients, except the cornflour (cornstarch) mixture, and beat well to blend. Pour into the pan and stir-fry for a further 1 minute or until it is heated through. Stir in the cornflour (cornstarch) mixture and cook, stirring constantly, until the sauce thickens and becomes translucent.

Remove the chicken pieces from the oven and pour over the sauce. Serve at once.

4 Servings

Sweet and Sour Chicken— another variation on the sweet and sour theme, this time with chicken as the meat.

Fish and Seafood

PAI CHIU TUNG LI YU
(Carp Steamed in White Wine)

The cooking liquid from this dish is traditionally served as a soup course in China.

	Metric/U.K.	U.S.
Carp, cleaned and gutted	1x1½kg/3lb	1x3lb
Water	150ml/5floz	⅝ cup
Beef stock	150ml/5floz	⅝ cup
Dry white wine	300ml/10floz	1¼ cups
Soy sauce	3 Tbs	3 Tbs
Sesame oil	1½ Tbs	1½ Tbs
Watercress, shredded	1 bunch	1 bunch
STUFFING		
Long-grain rice, soaked in cold water for 30 minutes and drained	4 Tbs	4 Tbs
Lean bacon, chopped	4 slices	4 slices
Spring onions (scallions), finely chopped	4	4
Chicken stock cube, crumbled	1	1
Fresh root ginger, peeled and chopped	7½cm/3in piece	3in piece
Salt and pepper to taste		

To make the stuffing, combine all the ingredients, then stuff the mixture into the carp. Close the cavity with a skewer or a trussing needle and thread.

Arrange the carp in a shallow oval-shaped heatproof casserole and pour over the water. Fill the bottom part of the double boiler or steamer to a depth of 5cm/2in with boiling water. Place the casserole in the top part of the boiler or steamer and cover. Place the boiler or steamer over moderate heat and steam for 45 minutes. Pour the stock and wine into the casserole and continue to steam for a further 45 minutes, or until the fish flakes easily.

Remove the boiler from the heat and lift out the casserole. Transfer the carp to a warmed, oval serving dish. Set aside and keep hot. Reserve the cooking liquid in the casserole. Combine the soy sauce and sesame oil and pour over the fish. Serve the fish at once.

If you wish to serve the cooking liquid as a soup course, stir the watercress into the cooking liquid. Place the casserole over moderate heat and bring to the boil, stirring frequently. Boil for 2 minutes. Remove from the heat and serve.

4-6 Servings

KUO TIEH YU PIEN
(Egg-Braised Sliced Fish)

If you wish to economize, use plaice (flounder) fillets instead of the sole suggested below.

	Metric/U.K.	U.S.
Sole fillets, cut into small strips about 5cm/2in x 2½cm/1in	½kg/1lb	1lb

Salt	2½ tsp	2½ tsp
Ground ginger	½ tsp	½ tsp
Cornflour (cornstarch)	1 Tbs	1 Tbs
Corn oil	1 Tbs	1 Tbs
Eggs, lightly beaten	3	3
Sufficient vegetable oil for deep-frying		
Sesame oil	75ml/3floz	⅜ cup
Chicken stock	50ml/2floz	¼ cup
Rice wine or dry sherry	2 Tbs	2 Tbs
Chopped parsley	1 Tbs	1 Tbs
Soy sauce	1½ Tbs	1½ Tbs
Lemon juice	1½ Tbs	1½ Tbs

Sprinkle the fish strips with 1½ teaspoons of salt, the ginger, cornflour (cornstarch) and corn oil, rubbing them into the flesh with your fingers. Set aside at room temperature for 1 hour.

Beat the eggs and remaining salt together, then set aside.

Fill a large saucepan one-third full with oil and heat until it reaches 185°C (360°F) on a deep-fat thermometer, or until a small cube of stale bread dropped into the oil turns golden in 50 seconds. Carefully lower the fish strips, a few at a time, into the oil and fry for 1½ minutes, or until they are lightly browned and crisp. Remove from the oil and drain on kitchen towels.

Heat the sesame oil in a large frying-pan. Add the fish strips to the pan, in one layer if possible, and fry for 1 minute. Pour in the beaten egg, tilting the pan so that the oil flows freely and the fish strips move and slide in the pan. When the egg is half-set, remove the pan from the heat and turn the fish strips over. Return the pan to the heat. When the egg has completely set, sprinkle over the chicken stock and wine or sherry. Turn the fish strips over once more and cook them in the liquid for 30 seconds.

Transfer the strips to a warmed serving dish, arranging them in one layer. Sprinkle over the remaining ingredients.

Serve at once.

4-6 Servings

Pai Chiu Tung Li Yu (carp steamed in white wine) makes an unusual centrepiece for dinner.

over and cook for a further 1 minute. Remove from the heat and pour off the excess oil.

To make the sauce, melt the fat in a small saucepan. Add the mushrooms and stir-fry for 1 minute. Add the wine, stock, sugar and salt, and bring to the boil. Stir in the cornflour (cornstarch) mixture and cook, stirring constantly, until the sauce thickens and becomes translucent. Remove from the heat and pour the sauce into the frying-pan. Stir carefully around the fish and return the pan to moderate heat. Cook, turning the fish pieces occasionally, for 2 minutes.

Transfer the fish pieces to a warmed serving dish. Pour over the sauce and serve at once.

6 Servings

Abalone is a favourite fish in China and it is used in a number of ways. Above the fish is pictured with its shells and right Pao Yu Tsa'ai Hsin stir-fried abalone and Chinese cabbage a popular dish based on abalone.

LIU YU-PIEN
(Sliced Fish in Wine Sauce)

	Metric/U.K.	U.S.
Sole fillets, cut into 5cm/2in x 2½cm/1in pieces	575g/1¼lb	1¼lb
Salt and pepper to taste		
Ground ginger	½ tsp	½ tsp
Cornflour (cornstarch)	2 tsp	2 tsp
Egg white, lightly beaten	1	1
Vegetable oil	75ml/3floz	⅜ cup
SAUCE Vegetable fat	2 tsp	2 tsp
Chinese dried mushrooms, soaked in cold water for 20 minutes, drained and chopped	8	8
Dry white wine	75ml/3floz	⅜ cup
Chicken stock	50ml/2floz	¼ cup
Sugar	1 tsp	1 tsp
Salt	½ tsp	½ tsp
Cornflour (cornstarch), blended with 3 Tbs water	2 tsp	2 tsp

Put the fish pieces on a board and rub them with salt, pepper, ground ginger and cornflour (cornstarch), rubbing them into the flesh with your fingers. Pour over the egg white and toss carefully to coat the pieces thoroughly.

Heat the oil in a large frying-pan. Add the fish pieces, in one layer if possible, and cook for 30 seconds, tilting the pan so that the oil flows freely around the fish. Turn the pieces

QUICK-FRIED ABALONE WITH MUSHROOMS

Abalone is a shellfish, very popular in Chinese cooking.

	Metric/U.K.	U.S.
Chicken stock	450ml/15floz	2 cups
Canned water chestnuts, drained and sliced	125g/4oz	4oz
Chinese dried mushrooms, soaked in cold water for 20 minutes, drained and sliced	8	8
Canned or fresh abalone, drained and thinly sliced	½kg/1lb	1lb
Spring onions (scallions), chopped	4	4
Soy sauce	2 Tbs	2 Tbs
Cornflour (cornstarch), blended with 2 Tbs water	1½ Tbs	1½ Tbs

Pour the stock into a deep frying-pan or saucepan and bring to the boil. Add the water chestnuts and mushrooms and reduce the heat to low. Simmer for 5 minutes. Add the abalone, spring onions (scallions) and soy sauce, and bring to the boil. Reduce the heat to low and simmer for a further 1 minute.

Stir in the cornflour (cornstarch) mixture and cook, stirring constantly, until the sauce thickens and becomes translucent. Transfer to a warmed serving bowl and serve at once.

4-6 Servings

PAO YU TS'AI HSIN
(Stir-fried Abalone and Chinese Cabbage)

	Metric/U.K.	U.S.
Peanut oil	3 Tbs	3 Tbs
Fresh root ginger, peeled and finely chopped	2½cm/1in piece	1in piece
Small leek, white part only, thinly sliced into rings	1	1
Small Chinese cabbage, shredded	1	1
Monosodium glutamate (MSG), (optional)	¼ tsp	¼ tsp
Salt and pepper to taste		
Soy sauce	2 tsp	2 tsp
Lemon juice	1½ Tbs	1½ Tbs
Canned or fresh abalone, drained and sliced	½kg/1lb	1lb

Heat the oil in a large, deep frying-pan. Add the ginger and leek and stir-fry for 2 minutes. Add the cabbage and stir-fry for 4 minutes, or until it is cooked through but still crisp. Sprinkle over the monosodium glutamate (MSG) if you are using it, salt, pepper, soy sauce and lemon juice and stir in the abalone. Cook the mixture, stirring constantly, for 5 minutes.

Transfer the mixture to a warmed serving dish and serve at once.

4-6 Servings

CANTONESE LOBSTER

This is one of the most popular Chinese dishes outside China and exemplifies Cantonese cooking. To be truly authentic, live lobsters should be used, but for convenience (and the squeamish!), the recipe has been adapted to the cooked lobsters obtainable at fish merchants or larger supermarkets. The traditional Chinese recipe is complicated in the extreme and is also very expensive—this recipe has therefore been slightly simplified.

	Metric/U.K.	U.S.
Cooked lobster, shell split, claws cracked and sac removed	1 x 1kg/2lb	1 x 2lb
Peanut oil	75ml/3floz	$\frac{3}{8}$ cup
Garlic cloves, crushed	2	2
Fresh root ginger, peeled and chopped	7½cm/3in piece	3in piece
Lean pork, minced (ground)	125g/4oz	4oz
Chicken stock	250ml/8floz	1 cup
Rice wine or dry sherry	1 Tbs	1 Tbs
Soy sauce	1 Tbs	1 Tbs
Monosodium glutamate (MSG), (optional)	¼ tsp	¼ tsp
Sugar	1 tsp	1 tsp
Cornflour (cornstarch), blended with 2 Tbs water	1 Tbs	1 Tbs
Spring onions (scallions), chopped	4	4
Eggs	2	2

Shrimps and prawns are abundant and popular in China and Deep-Fried Prawns or Shrimps is one particularly superb yet simple way of serving them.

Chop the lobster into pieces and set aside. (You can, if you wish, remove the shell but it is traditional to cook this dish with the shell on.)

Heat half the oil in a large, deep frying-pan. Add the garlic and stir-fry for 1 minute. Add the lobster pieces to the pan and stir-fry for 3 to 5 minutes, or until they are heated through. Transfer to a warmed serving dish and keep hot while you make the sauce.

Heat the remaining oil in the same frying-pan. Add the ginger and pork and fry until the pork loses all its pinkness. Pour over the stock and bring to the boil. Combine the wine or sherry, soy sauce, monosodium glutamate (MSG) and sugar, then stir the mixture into the pan. Stir-fry for 1 minute. Stir in the cornflour (cornstarch) mixture and cook, stirring constantly, until the sauce thickens and becomes translucent. Stir in the spring onions (scallions) and cook for 1 minute, stirring.

Turn off the heat and beat the eggs a few times just to combine them. Gently pour over the mixture, stirring and lifting the sides of the mixture to allow the egg to run over and under. When the egg mixture becomes creamy and slightly 'set', spoon the sauce over the lobster. Serve at once.

2-4 Servings

BEAN CURD WITH CRABMEAT

	Metric/U.K.	U.S.
Fresh bean curd	3 cakes	3 cakes
Groundnut oil	3 Tbs	3 Tbs
Spring onions (scallions), chopped	2	2
Fresh root ginger, peeled and chopped	5cm/2in piece	2in piece
Salt	1½ tsp	1½ tsp
Chicken stock	3 Tbs	3 Tbs
Crabmeat, with the shell and cartilage removed and flaked	225g/8oz	8oz
Cornflour (cornstarch), blended with 5 tsp water	½ tsp	½ tsp
Watercress sprigs	5	5

Slice each bean curd cake into ½cm/¼in slices, then cut each slice in half.

Heat a heavy frying-pan over high heat for 30 seconds. Add the oil, tilting the pan so that it covers the bottom completely, and heat for 30 seconds. Reduce the heat to moderately high. Add the spring onions (scallions) and ginger and stir-fry for 1 minute. Add the bean curd, salt and stock, and bring to the boil. Cover and cook for 3 minutes. Stir in the crabmeat and cook for 1 minute. Stir in the cornflour (cornstarch) and cook, stirring constantly, until the liquid has thickened and become translucent.

Transfer the mixture to a warmed serving dish, garnish with the watercress and serve at once.

4 Servings

DEEP-FRIED PRAWNS OR SHRIMPS

	Metric/U.K.	U.S.
Tomato purée (paste)	3 Tbs	3 Tbs
Soy sauce	2 Tbs	2 Tbs
Chilli sauce	1 tsp	1 tsp
Sugar	1 tsp	1 tsp
Large prawns or shrimps	700g/1½lb	1½lb
Egg, lightly beaten	1	1
Flour	3 Tbs	3 Tbs
Cornflour (cornstarch)	2 tsp	2 tsp
Fresh root ginger, peeled and finely chopped	2½cm/1in piece	1in piece
Salt	½ tsp	½ tsp
Water	75ml/3floz	⅜ cup
Sufficient vegetable oil for deep-frying		

Combine the tomato purée (paste), soy sauce, chilli sauce and sugar together, then pour into a sauceboat. Set aside.

Remove the shells from the prawns or shrimps, leaving the tails intact. Under cold running water, gently remove the black veins from the flesh, then drain on kitchen towels.

Put the beaten egg into a bowl and beat in the flour, cornflour (cornstarch), ginger, salt and water until the mixture forms a smooth batter.

Fill a large saucepan one-third full with oil and heat until it reaches 180°C (350°F) on a deep-fat thermometer, or until a small cube of stale bread dropped into the oil turns golden in 55 seconds. Holding the prawns or shrimps by the tails, dip each one in the batter, then arrange them, a few at a time, in a deep-frying basket. Carefully lower the basket into the oil and fry for 2 to 3 minutes, or until they are golden brown. Remove from the oil and drain the prawns or shrimps on kitchen towels.

Transfer to a serving dish and serve at once, with the sauce.

4-6 Servings

QUICK-FRIED SHRIMPS, CHICKEN AND PETITS POIS

	Metric/U.K.	U.S.
Vegetable oil	2 Tbs	2 Tbs
Cooked chicken meat, cut into small cubes	225g/8oz	8oz
Ground ginger	½ tsp	½ tsp
Frozen petits pois, thawed	½kg/1lb	1lb
Small frozen shrimps, thawed	175g/6oz	6oz
Butter	25g/1oz	2 Tbs
Chicken stock cube, crumbled	½	½

Water	75ml/3floz	$\frac{3}{8}$ cup
Rice wine or dry sherry	2 Tbs	2 Tbs
Soy sauce	1 Tbs	1 Tbs
Soft brown sugar	1 Tbs	1 Tbs
Cornflour (cornstarch), blended with 3 Tbs water	1 Tbs	1 Tbs

Quick-Fried Shrimps on Crackling Rice is rich, delicious and very filling. 'Crackling' rice is so called because, after being deep-fried, it 'crackles' as the sauce is poured over.

Heat the oil in a saucepan. Add the chicken cubes and ginger and stir-fry for 1 minute. Add the petits pois, shrimps and butter and stir-fry for a further 30 seconds. Add the stock cube, water, wine or sherry, soy sauce and sugar, and bring to the boil, stirring constantly. Stir-fry for a further 30 seconds.

Stir in the cornflour (cornstarch) mixture and cook, stirring constantly, until the sauce thickens and becomes translucent. Remove from the heat and transfer the mixture to a warmed serving dish. Serve at once.

4 Servings

STIR-FRIED SHRIMPS WITH CASHEWS

	Metric/U.K.	U.S.
Small shelled shrimps	$\frac{1}{2}$kg/1lb	1lb
Rice wine or dry sherry	1 Tbs	1 Tbs
Egg white, lightly beaten	1	1
Cornflour (cornstarch)	$1\frac{1}{2}$ Tbs	$1\frac{1}{2}$ Tbs

	Metric/U.K.	U.S.
Salt and pepper to taste		
Ground ginger	½ tsp	½ tsp
Vegetable oil	50ml/2floz	¼ cup
Unsalted cashew nuts	125g/4oz	1 cup
Fresh root ginger, peeled and finely chopped	5cm/2in piece	2in piece
Spring onions (scallions), finely chopped	4	4
Canned bamboo shoot, drained and finely chopped	75g/3oz	3oz

Put the shrimps into a shallow bowl. Combine half the wine or sherry, the egg white, 1 tablespoon of cornflour (cornstarch), seasoning and ground ginger until the mixture forms a smooth batter. Pour the batter over the shrimps and toss gently to coat them thoroughly. Set aside to marinate for 30 minutes.

Heat the oil in a large, deep frying-pan. Add the cashews and fry, turning occasionally, for 5 minutes or until they are deep golden. Push them to the side of the pan and add the shrimps. Stir-fry for 3 minutes or until they are crisp. Stir in the remaining ingredients except the remaining wine or sherry and cornflour (cornstarch). Stir-fry for 2 minutes. Stir in the remaining wine or sherry and cornflour (cornstarch) and stir the cashews back into the shrimp mixture. Cook until the sauce thickens and becomes translucent.

Transfer the mixture to a warmed serving dish and serve at once.

6 Servings

QUICK-FRIED SHRIMPS ON CRACKLING RICE

	Metric/U.K.	U.S.
Shelled shrimps	225g/8oz	8oz
Boned chicken breast, cut into cubes	225g/8oz	8oz
Salt	2 tsp	2 tsp
White pepper	1 tsp	1 tsp
Cornflour (cornstarch)	1 Tbs	1 Tbs
Cooked rice	450g/1lb	6 cups
Sufficient vegetable oil for deep-frying		

SAUCE		
Vegetable oil	2 Tbs	2 Tbs
Onion, very finely chopped	1	1
Beef stock	150ml/5floz	⅝ cup
Tomato purée (paste)	2 Tbs	2 Tbs
Soy sauce	1½ Tbs	1½ Tbs
Sugar	1½ Tbs	1½ Tbs
Wine vinegar	1½ Tbs	1½ Tbs
Rice wine or dry sherry	2 Tbs	2 Tbs
Chilli sauce	1 tsp	1 tsp
Cornflour (cornstarch)	4 tsp	4 tsp

Pre-heat the oven to very cool 140°C (Gas Mark 1, 275°F).

Sprinkle the shrimps and chicken cubes with the salt, pepper and cornflour (cornstarch), rubbing them into the flesh with your fingers.

Place the rice in an ovenproof dish and put the dish into the oven. Dry out the rice for 15 to 20 minutes, or until it is slightly crisp.

Meanwhile, to make the sauce, heat the oil in a large frying-pan. Add the onion and fry until it is soft. Stir in all the remaining ingredients and bring to the boil. Cook the sauce, stirring constantly, until it thickens and becomes translucent. Remove the pan from the heat and set aside.

Fill a large saucepan one-third full with oil and heat until it reaches 185°C (360°F) on a deep-fat thermometer, or until a small cube of stale bread dropped into the oil turns golden in 50 seconds. Put the shrimps and chicken cubes in a deep-frying basket and carefully lower them into the oil. Fry for 1 minute. Remove from the oil and drain on kitchen towels. Transfer the shrimps and chicken cubes to the sauce in the saucepan and return the pan to moderate heat. Cook, stirring constantly, for 2 minutes.

Meanwhile, return the saucepan containing the oil to moderate heat and heat until the oil reaches 180°C (350°F) on a deep-fat thermometer, or until a small cube of stale bread dropped into the oil turns golden in 55 seconds. Remove the rice from the oven and arrange it in a narrow-meshed deep-frying basket. Carefully lower the basket into the oil and fry the rice for 1½ minutes. Remove from the oil and drain on kitchen towels.

Arrange the rice on a warmed serving dish and pour over the shrimp mixture and sauce. Serve at once.

4-6 Servings

SHRIMP FRITTERS

	Metric/U.K.	U.S.
Shrimps, shelled, with the tails left on and de-veined	700g/1½lb	1½lb
Cornflour (cornstarch)	6 Tbs	6 Tbs
Salt	1 tsp	1 tsp
Cayenne pepper	¼ tsp	¼ tsp
Eggs, separated	2	2
Water	3 Tbs	3 Tbs
Sufficient vegetable oil for deep-frying		
SAUCE Wine vinegar	1 Tbs	1 Tbs
Soft brown sugar	1 Tbs	1 Tbs
Tomato purée (paste)	1 Tbs	1 Tbs
Soy sauce	1 Tbs	1 Tbs
Vegetable oil	1 Tbs	1 Tbs
Salt	¼ tsp	¼ tsp
Rice wine or dry sherry	50ml/2floz	¼ cup
Cornflour (cornstarch), blended with 125ml/ 4floz water	1 Tbs	1 Tbs
Lemons, cut into wedges	2	2

Wash the shrimps in cold water then drain on kitchen towels.

Combine the cornflour (cornstarch), salt and cayenne together. Make a well in the centre and add the egg yolks and water. Beat gently until the mixture forms a smooth batter. Set aside for 20 minutes.

Meanwhile make the sauce. Put all the ingredients, except the cornflour (cornstarch) mixture and lemons, into a saucepan and bring to the boil, stirring constantly. Reduce the heat to low and stir in the cornflour (cornstarch) mixture. Cook, stirring constantly, until the sauce thickens and is smooth. Remove from the heat and set aside.

Beat the egg whites until they form stiff peaks. Quickly fold them into the egg yolk batter.

Fill a large saucepan one-third full with oil and heat until it reaches 190°C (375°F) on a deep-fat thermomemter, or until a small cube of stale bread dropped into the oil turns golden in 40 seconds. Holding the shrimps by the tails, dip each one in the batter then drop carefully into the oil. Fry, a few at a time, for

3 to 4 minutes, or until they are golden brown. Remove from the oil and drain on kitchen towels.

Arrange the fritters on a warmed serving dish and garnish with the lemon wedges. Reheat the sauce, then pour into small individual bowls. Serve at once, with the fritters.

6-8 Servings

HWANG CHI HSIA REN
(Shrimps in Tomato Sauce)

	Metric/U.K.	U.S.
Shelled shrimps	½kg/1lb	1lb
Salt	1 tsp	1 tsp
Ground ginger	¼ tsp	¼ tsp
Cornflour (cornstarch)	1½ tsp	1½ tsp
Vegetable oil	75ml/3floz	⅜ cup
SAUCE Butter	1½ Tbs	1½ Tbs
Medium tomatoes, blanched, peeled and quartered	3	3
Soy sauce	2½ Tbs	2½ Tbs
Tomato purée (paste)	2 Tbs	2 Tbs
Cornflour (cornstarch)	2 tsp	2 tsp
Chicken stock	75ml/3floz	⅜ cup
Rice wine or dry sherry	2 Tbs	2 Tbs
Sugar	1 tsp	1 tsp

Put the shrimps in a shallow dish. Sprinkle over the salt, ginger and cornflour (cornstarch), rubbing them into the flesh with your fingers. Heat the oil in a large frying-pan. Add the shrimps and fry for 2 minutes, stirring constantly. Transfer the shrimps to a plate, cover and keep hot. Pour off the excess oil from the pan and return it to moderate heat. Add the butter. When it melts, add the tomatoes and stir-fry for 2 minutes. Add the soy sauce and tomato purée (paste) and stir-fry for a further 30 seconds.

Combine the cornflour (cornstarch), stock, wine or sherry and sugar. Pour the mixture into the frying-pan and cook, stirring constantly, until the sauce thickens and becomes translucent. Return the shrimps to the sauce and coat them thoroughly. Stir-fry for a further 1½ minutes.

Transfer the mixture to a warmed serving dish and serve at once.

4-6 Servings

WINTER PRAWNS OR SHRIMPS

	Metric/U.K.	U.S.
Egg whites	10	10
Cornflour (cornstarch)	2 tsp	2 tsp
Salt	½ tsp	½ tsp
Shelled prawns or shrimps	175g/6oz	6oz
Sufficient vegetable oil for deep-frying		
Monosodium glutamate (MSG), (optional)	¼ tsp	¼ tsp
Cooked chicken, minced (ground)	50g/2oz	2oz
Chopped chives	2 Tbs	2 Tbs

Beat 1 egg white, the cornflour (cornstarch) and salt together until they form a smooth paste. Arrange the prawns or shrimps in the paste and stir gently until they are coated.

Fill a large saucepan one-third full with oil and heat until it reaches 185°C (360°F) on a deep-fat thermometer, or until a small cube of stale bread dropped into the oil turns golden brown in 50 seconds. Put the prawns or shrimps in a deep-frying basket and carefully lower them into the oil. Fry for 1 minute. Remove from the oil and drain on kitchen towels. Set aside.

Beat the remaining egg whites with the monosodium glutamate (MSG), if you are using it, until they form stiff peaks. Pile half the mixture on a dish and arrange the prawns or shrimps over it. Using a spatula, gently and carefully spread the remaining egg white mixture over the prawns or shrimps.

Tilt the dish over the saucepan containing the hot oil and very carefully slide the egg and prawn or shrimp mixture into the oil. Fry the mixture for 3 minutes, basting the top with oil if it is not fully covered. Remove the pan from the heat and carefully lift out the mixture. Drain on kitchen towels, then transfer to a warmed serving dish.

Sprinkle over the chicken and chives and serve at once.

4-6 Servings

Unusual, delicate, fabulous to eat, Winter Prawns or Shrimps.

Vegetables and rice

CHOW BARG CHOY (Fried Cabbage)

	Metric/U.K.	U.S.
Vegetable oil	2 Tbs	2 Tbs
Garlic clove, crushed	1	1
Chinese cabbage, shredded	700g/1½lb	1½lb
Water	75ml/3floz	⅜ cup
Soy sauce	2 tsp	2 tsp
Flour	1 tsp	1 tsp
Sugar	½ tsp	½ tsp

Heat the oil in a large frying-pan. Add the garlic and stir-fry for 1 minute. Add the cabbage and cook for 6 minutes, stirring.

Mix the water, soy sauce and flour together to form a smooth paste. Stir in the sugar then stir into the pan. Stir-fry for 2 minutes.

Serve at once.

4-6 Servings

HUNG SHAO PAI TS'AI
(Red-Cooked Cabbage)

	Metric/U.K.	U.S.
Butter	40g/1½oz	3 Tbs
Vegetable oil	3 Tbs	3 Tbs
Chinese cabbage, shredded	1	1
Sugar	3½ tsp	3½ tsp
Soy sauce	5 Tbs	5 Tbs
Water	3 Tbs	3 Tbs
Chicken stock cube, crumbled	½	½
Rice wine or dry sherry	3 Tbs	3 Tbs

Melt the butter with the oil in a large frying-pan. Add the cabbage and, using wooden spoons, turn the cabbage in the oil mixture until it is thoroughly coated. Reduce the heat to low, cover and simmer for 5 minutes.

Stir in the sugar, soy sauce, water, stock cube, wine or sherry and simmer, covered, for a further 5 minutes.

Transfer the mixture to a warmed serving dish and serve at once.

6 Servings

NAI-YU-TS'AI HSIN
(Chinese Cabbage in Cream Sauce)

	Metric/U.K.	U.S.
Butter	1 Tbs	1 Tbs
Sesame oil	1 Tbs	1 Tbs
Spring onions (scallions), thinly sliced	3	3

Small Chinese cabbages, coarsely shredded	2	2
Salt and pepper to taste		
White wine vinegar	1 Tbs	1 Tbs
Single (light) cream	125ml/4floz	½ cup
Soy sauce	2 tsp	2 tsp

Melt the butter with the oil in a large frying-pan. Add the spring onions (scallions) and cabbages and stir-fry for 3 minutes. Sprinkle over the salt, pepper and vinegar and stir-fry for a further 3 minutes, or until the cabbage is cooked but still crisp.

Stir in the remaining ingredients and cook, stirring constantly, for 4 minutes, or until the sauce comes to the boil. Remove from the heat and transfer the mixture to a warmed serving dish. Serve at once.

6 Servings

BEAN SPROUTS WITH GINGER

	Metric/U.K.	U.S.
Vegetable oil	3 Tbs	3 Tbs
Large onion, thinly sliced	1	1
Fresh root ginger, peeled and finely chopped	2½cm/1in piece	1in piece
Salt	1 tsp	1 tsp
Bean sprouts	½kg/1lb	1lb

Heat the oil in a large frying-pan. Add the onion and fry until it is soft. Add the ginger and stir-fry for 3 minutes. Stir in the remaining ingredients, increase the heat to moderately high and stir-fry for 3 minutes, or until the bean sprouts are cooked through but still crisp.

Two fine examples of Fukien food, where the 'red cooking' technique using lots of soy sauce is traditional. On the left Hung Shao-Ngiu Jou (red-cooked beef with star anise—recipe page 23) and Hung Shao Pai Ts'ai (red-cooked cabbage). Top right: Bok Choy or Chinese cabbage. Bottom right: Bean curd, in dried lengths and in its usual form used extensively in Chinese cooking, soft white cakes about 7½cm/ 3in square.

Transfer to a warmed serving dish and serve at once.

4-6 Servings

FRIED CUCUMBER AND PINEAPPLE

	Metric/U.K.	U.S.
Vegetable oil	2 Tbs	2 Tbs
Small cucumbers, thinly sliced crosswise	2	2
Salt	$\frac{1}{2}$ tsp	$\frac{1}{2}$ tsp
Vinegar	1 Tbs	1 Tbs
Canned pineapple chunks, drained	225g/8oz	8oz
Water	175ml/6floz	$\frac{3}{4}$ cup
Flour	2 tsp	2 tsp
Sugar	1 tsp	1 tsp
Soy sauce	1 tsp	1 tsp

Heat the oil in a frying-pan. Add the cucumber slices, salt and vinegar and cook for 4 minutes, stirring frequently. Add the pineapple to the pan and cook for a further 2 minutes, stirring occasionally.

Beat the water, flour, sugar and soy sauce together until the mixture is smooth. Pour into the frying-pan and bring to the boil, stirring constantly. Cook for a further 4 minutes, stirring occasionally.

Transfer the mixture to a warmed serving dish and serve at once.

4-6 Servings

BAMBOO SHOOT WITH MUSHROOMS

	Metric/U.K.	U.S.
Groundnut oil	50ml/2floz	$\frac{1}{4}$ cup
Canned bamboo shoot, drained and sliced	350g/12oz	12oz
Chinese dried mushrooms, soaked in cold water for 20 minutes, drained and chopped	12	12
Rice wine or dry sherry	2 Tbs	2 Tbs
Soy sauce	4 Tbs	4 Tbs

Sugar	1 Tbs	1 Tbs
Monosodium glutamate (MSG), (optional)	$\frac{1}{4}$ tsp	$\frac{1}{4}$ tsp
Water	75ml/3floz	$\frac{3}{8}$ cup

Heat a heavy-based frying-pan over moderately high heat for 30 seconds. Add the oil and swirl it around the pan. Add the bamboo shoot and mushrooms and stir-fry for 5 minutes. Stir in the remaining ingredients and reduce the heat to low. Cover the pan and simmer for 5 minutes.

Transfer the mixture to a warmed serving dish and serve at once.

4-6 Servings

FRIED MIXED VEGETABLES

	Metric/U.K.	U.S.
Vegetable oil	3 Tbs	3 Tbs
Garlic clove, crushed	1	1
Fresh root ginger, peeled and finely chopped	2$\frac{1}{2}$cm/1in piece	1in piece
Salt and pepper to taste		
Carrots, thinly sliced on the diagonal	2	2
Small green pepper, pith and seeds removed and chopped	1	1
Very small cauliflower, broken into small flowerets	1	1
Bean sprouts	50g/2oz	2oz
Chicken stock	150ml/5floz	$\frac{5}{8}$ cup
Soy sauce	2 tsp	2 tsp
Soft brown sugar	1 tsp	1 tsp

Heat the oil in a large frying-pan. Add the garlic, ginger, salt and pepper, and stir-fry for 1 minute. Add the carrots and stir-fry for 1 minute. Add the green pepper and cauliflower and stir-fry for 3 minutes. Add the bean sprouts and stir-fry for 1 minute. Stir in the remaining ingredients and bring to the boil. Reduce the heat to low, cover and simmer for a further 4 minutes.

Transfer the mixture to a warmed serving dish and serve at once.

4-6 Servings

STIR-FRIED MIXED VEGETABLES WITH WATER CHESTNUTS

This dish has a delightfully crunchy flavour. If mange-tout (snow peas) are not available, green or French beans may be substituted. Bamboo shoot and water chestnuts may be obtained from Chinese provision stores.

	Metric/U.K.	U.S.
Vegetable oil	50ml/2floz	¼ cup
Fresh root ginger, peeled and finely chopped	5cm/2in piece	2in piece
Mange-tout (snow peas), cut into 5cm/2in lengths	½kg/1lb	1lb
Canned bamboo shoot, drained and sliced	50g/2oz	2oz
Water chestnuts, sliced	4	4
Rice wine or dry sherry	1 Tbs	1 Tbs
Sugar	¼ tsp	¼ tsp

Heat the oil in a large frying-pan. Add the ginger and stir-fry for 30 seconds. Add the mange-tout (snow peas) and bamboo shoot and stir-fry for 4 minutes. Stir in all of the remaining ingredients until they are thoroughly mixed.

Transfer the mixture to a warmed serving dish and serve at once.

4-6 Servings

BEAN CURD WITH SPICY MEAT AND VEGETABLES

This dish is an adaptation of one of the more fiery dishes from the Szechuan province of China.

	Metric/U.K.	U.S.
Peanut oil	50ml/2floz	¼ cup
Garlic clove, crushed	1	1
Fresh root ginger, peeled and finely chopped	7½cm/3in piece	3in piece
Spring onions (scallions), finely chopped	4	4
Chinese dried mushrooms, soaked in cold water for 20 minutes, drained and chopped	4	4
Red pepper flakes	1 tsp	1 tsp
Dried red chillis, chopped	2	2
Minced (ground) beef	175g/6oz	6oz
Soy sauce	2 Tbs	2 Tbs
Chicken stock	250ml/8floz	1 cup
Fresh bean curd, mashed	3 cakes	3 cakes
Cornflour (cornstarch), blended with 2 Tbs chicken stock	1 Tbs	1 Tbs

Heat the oil in a large saucepan. Add the garlic, ginger, spring onions (scallions) and mushrooms, and stir-fry for 3 minutes. Stir in the red pepper flakes and chillis and stir-fry for a further 1 minute. Add the minced (ground) meat and fry until it loses its pinkness. Pour over the soy sauce and stock and bring to the boil, stirring constantly. Stir in the mashed bean curd and stir-fry for 5 minutes. Add the cornflour (cornstarch) mixture and cook, stirring constantly, until the sauce thickens.

Transfer the mixture to a warmed serving dish and serve at once.

6-8 Servings

SWEET AND SOUR VEGETABLES

The basic sweet and sour sauce is usually served with pork, chicken or fish in the west, but it can be served with vegetables, too, and the result is delicious.

	Metric/U.K.	U.S.
Peanut oil	50ml/2floz	¼ cup
Carrots, thinly sliced on the diagonal	3	3
Bamboo shoot, drained and sliced	50g/2oz	2oz
Leek, white part only, thinly sliced on the diagonal	1	1
Green pepper, pith and seeds removed and thinly sliced	1	1
Bean sprouts	125g/4oz	4oz
Pineapple juice and water mixed	250ml/8floz	1 cup

	Metric/U.K.	U.S.
Wine vinegar	2 Tbs	2 Tbs
Soy sauce	1½ Tbs	1½ Tbs
Soft brown sugar	2 Tbs	2 Tbs
Cornflour (cornstarch), blended with 2 Tbs water	2 Tbs	2 Tbs

Heat the oil in a large frying-pan. Add the vegetables and stir-fry for 5 minutes. Combine the pineapple juice, vinegar, soy sauce and sugar together and blend well. Pour over the vegetables and bring to the boil. Cook for 2 minutes, stirring occasionally. Stir in the cornflour (cornstarch) mixture and cook, stirring constantly, until the sauce thickens and becomes translucent.

Transfer the mixture to a warmed serving dish and serve at once.

4-6 Servings

BASIC BOILED RICE

	Metric/U.K.	U.S.
Long-grain rice, soaked in cold water for 30 minutes and drained	225g/8oz	1⅓ cups
Water	450ml/15floz	2 cups
Salt	1 tsp	1 tsp

Put the rice into a saucepan and pour over the water and salt. Bring to the boil, reduce the heat to low and cover the pan. Simmer for 15 to 20 minutes, or until the rice is cooked and tender. Serve.

4 Servings

BASIC FRIED RICE

	Metric/U.K.	U.S.
Long-grain rice, soaked in cold water for 30 minutes and drained	225g/8oz	1⅓ cups
Water	450ml/15floz	2 cups
Salt	1 tsp	1 tsp
Peanut oil	2 Tbs	2 Tbs
Soy sauce	2 tsp	2 tsp

Put the rice into a saucepan and pour over the water and salt. Bring to the boil, reduce the

heat to low and cover the pan. Simmer for 15 to 20 minutes, or until the water has been absorbed and the rice is cooked and tender. Remove from the heat.

Heat the oil in a large frying-pan. Add the rice and cook for 1 minute, stirring constantly to coat the rice with the oil. Stir in half the soy sauce and fry, stirring constantly, until the rice is lightly browned. Remove from the heat and stir in the remaining soy sauce.

Transfer to a warmed serving dish and serve at once.

4 Servings

CHOW FARN
(Fried Rice)

This is one of the basic dishes of Chinese cuisine and can be either served on its own, or used as an elaborate rice accompaniment dish.

	Metric/U.K.	U.S.
Long-grain rice, soaked in cold water for 30 minutes and drained	225g/8oz	1⅓ cups
Water	450ml/15floz	2 cups
Salt	1½ tsp	1½ tsp
Vegetable oil	2 Tbs	2 Tbs
Medium onions, finely chopped	2	2
Cooked ham, finely chopped	225g/8oz	8oz
Petits pois	2 Tbs	2 Tbs
Medium tomatoes, blanched, peeled and quartered	2	2
Frozen shrimps, thawed and shelled	225g/8oz	8oz
Soy sauce	1 Tbs	1 Tbs
Egg, lightly beaten	1	1

Put the rice into a saucepan and pour over the water and 1 teaspoon of salt. Bring to the boil, reduce the heat to low and cover the pan. Simmer for 15 to 20 minutes, or until the water has been absorbed and the rice is cooked and tender. Remove from the heat.

Heat the oil in a large saucepan. Add the onions and fry until they are soft. Stir in the ham, petits pois, tomatoes, shrimps and remaining salt and cook for 1 minute, stirring

constantly. Stir in the cooked rice and cook for 2 minutes, stirring constantly. Add the soy sauce and egg and cook for 2 minutes, stirring constantly.

Transfer the mixture to a warmed serving dish and serve at once.

4-6 Servings

HAM FRIED RICE

	Metric/U.K.	U.S.
Long-grain rice, soaked in cold water for 30 minutes and drained	225g/8oz	1¼ cups
Water	450ml/15floz	2 cups
Salt	1 tsp	1 tsp
Butter	15g/½oz	1 Tbs
Eggs, lightly beaten	2	2
Vegetable oil	50ml/2floz	¼ cup
Green beans, cut into 2½cm/1in lengths	125g/4oz	4oz
Cooked ham, diced	275g/10oz	10oz
Black pepper	½ tsp	½ tsp
Spring onions (scallions)	4	4

Put the rice into a saucepan and pour over the water and 1 teaspoon of salt. Bring to the boil, reduce the heat to low and cover the pan. Simmer for 15 to 20 minutes or until the water has been absorbed and the rice is cooked and tender. Remove from the heat.

Melt the butter in a large frying-pan. Add the eggs and cook for 2 to 3 minutes, or until they are set on the underside. Stir the eggs and cook for 2 to 3 minutes more or until they are just set. Remove from the heat and transfer the eggs to a bowl, breaking them up with a fork. Set aside.

Add the oil to the frying-pan and heat over moderately high heat. Add the cooked rice, beans, ham and pepper, and cook for 2 minutes, stirring constantly. Reduce the heat to moderately low and add the spring onions (scallions) and eggs. Cook for 2 minutes, stirring constantly, or until the mixture is very hot.

Transfer the mixture to a warmed serving dish and serve at once.

4 Servings

Fried rice can be very basic or plain, or it can be very complex and rich. Ham Fried Rice could be served as a light meal on its own rather than as an accompaniment to meat or fish dishes.

Sweets

WONTONS WITH ALMONDS AND DATES

The Chinese rarely eat desserts as they are known in the west, but they are fond of sweetmeats, and this wonton sweetmeat stuffed with fruit, nuts and finely grated orange rind is a particular favourite. A recipe for basic wonton dough is given on page 8.

	Metric/U.K.	U.S.
Stoned dates, finely chopped	175g/6oz	1 cup
Slivered almonds	50g/2oz	⅓ cup
Sesame seeds	2 tsp	2 tsp
Finely grated rind of 1 orange		
Orange-flower water	2 Tbs	2 Tbs
Wonton dough, thinly rolled and cut into 36 squares or 36 bought wonton wrappers	225g/8oz	8oz
Sufficient vegetable oil for deep-frying		
Icing (confectioners') sugar	2 Tbs	2 Tbs
Orange, thinly sliced	1	1

Put the dates, almonds, sesame seeds, orange rind and orange-flower water in a bowl and knead the mixture until the ingredients are thoroughly combined.

Lay the wonton wrappers on a flat surface and put a little filling just below the centre. Wet the edges of the dough, then fold over one corner to make a triangle, pinching the edges together to seal. Pull the corners at the base of the triangle together and pinch to seal.

Fill a large saucepan one-third full with oil and heat until it reaches 190°C (375°F) on a deep-fat thermometer, or until a small cube of stale bread dropped into the oil turns golden in 40 seconds. Carefully lower the wontons into the oil, a few at a time, and fry for 2 minutes, or until they are golden brown and crisp. Remove from the oil and drain on kitchen towels.

Arrange the cooked wontons on a warmed serving dish. Sprinkle over the icing (confectioners') sugar and garnish with the orange slices.

Serve at once.

4-6 Servings

Wontons can be sweet as well as savoury and can be served as sweetmeats as well as dim sum. Wontons with Almonds and Dates are crisp, deep-fried packets of wonton dough stuffed with nuts and fruit.

HONEY APPLES

One of the favourite Chinese desserts both inside China and outside, Honey Apples is apple rings dipped in syrup then in batter and finally deep-fried.

	Metric/U.K.	U.S.
Cooking apples, peeled, cored and cut into 4 rings	5	5
SYRUP		
Soft brown sugar	125g/4oz	⅔ cup
Clear honey	4 Tbs	4 Tbs
Water	250ml/8floz	1 cup
Juice of 2 lemons		
BATTER		
Flour	125g/4oz	1 cup

Salt	¼ tsp	¼ tsp
Sugar	2 tsp	2 tsp
Egg yolks	3	3
Water	175ml/6floz	¾ cup
Egg whites, stiffly beaten	3	3
Sufficient vegetable oil for deep-frying		
DECORATION		
Icing (confectioners') sugar	75g/3oz	¾ cup
Lemon, sliced	1	1

To make the syrup, put the sugar, honey and water into a large saucepan. Bring to the boil, then boil for 5 minutes. Remove from the heat and stir in the lemon juice. Drop the apple rings into the syrup and, using a wooden spoon, carefully stir the apples to coat the rings thoroughly with the syrup. Set aside for 1 hour.

Meanwhile, make the batter. Sift the flour and salt into a bowl and stir in the sugar. Beat in the egg yolks and water until the mixture forms a smooth batter. Quickly fold in the egg whites. Using a slotted spoon, transfer the apple rings to the batter, and stir to coat them completely. Discard the syrup. Set the apples aside.

Fill a large saucepan one-third full with oil and heat until it reaches 180°C (350°F) on a deep-fat thermometer, or until a small cube of stale bread dropped into the oil turns golden in 55 seconds. Carefully lower the apple rings into the oil, a few at a time, and fry for 2 to 3 minutes, or until they are golden brown and crisp. Remove from the oil and drain on kitchen towels.

Put the icing (confectioners') sugar on a large plate. Dip the apples in the sugar and arrange them on a warmed serving dish. Decorate with the lemon slices and serve at once.

6-8 Servings

MELON SHELLS FILLED WITH FRUIT

	Metric/U.K.	U.S.
Melon, cut in half lengthways	1	1
Canned lychees, drained	20	20

	Metric/U.K.	U.S.
Peaches, blanched, peeled and sliced	4	4
White grapes, peeled and seeded	½kg/1lb	1lb

Melon Shells Filled with Fruit makes a refreshing end to a Chinese meal.

Carefully scoop out the flesh of the melon and cut it into cubes, removing as many seeds as possible. Transfer the diced flesh to a bowl. Add the remaining ingredients and carefully and gently toss the mixture to mix the fruit.

Divide the mixture equally between the two melon shells. Put the shells into the refrigerator to chill for 30 minutes.

Serve at once.

6 Servings